RELIGIOUS INSTRUCTION

IN THE

NATIONAL SCHOOLS OF SCOTLAND.

FULL REPORT

OF THE

GREAT PUBLIC MEETING

HELD IN THE QUEEN'S HALL, STRANRAER.

ON WEDNESDAY EVENING, 24TH JANUARY 1872.

The following Gentlemen took part in the proceedings :—

Dr JOHN ORGILL, Stranraer.
Rev. WM. TURNBULL, Glasgow.
Rev. THOMAS BARTY, Kirkcolm.
WM. KIDSTON, Esq. of Ferniegair.
JOHN GORDON, Esq., Stranraer.
Dr DAVID EASTON, Stranraer.

Rev. Dr BEGG, Edinburgh.
JOHN M'CLEW, Esq., Dinvin.
JOHN GIBB, Esq., Stranraer.
Rev. WM. M. JOHNSTONE, Stranraer.
WM. CUMMING, Esq., Kirkcolm.
Rev. JOHN STURROCK, Stranraer.

Rev. T. EASTON, Stranraer.

Mark J. Stewart, Esq., yr. of Southwick, in the Chair.

ALSO

REPORT OF AN ADDRESS

BY THE REV. T. EASTON,

IN REVIEW OF THE LORD ADVOCATE'S SPEECH AT STRANRAER.

(Reprinted from the " Galloway Gazette.")

INDEX TO SPEECHES.

APPENDIX.

Scotch Education Bill.

PUBLIC MEETING AT STRANRAER.

A CROWDED and most enthusiastic public meeting was held in the Queen's Hall, Stranraer, on Wednesday evening, the 24th January, "for advocating the legislative continuance of religious instruction in National Schools." Upwards of a hundred persons were unable to find either standing or sitting room, and had to go home disappointed. On the platform were:—Mark J. Stewart, Esq., yr. of Southwick; Rev. Dr Begg, Edinburgh; Rev. Mr Turnbull, Glasgow; William Kidston, Esq. of Ferniegair; Major-General Birch, Dunskey; Rev. Messrs Easton, Sturrock, and Johnston, Stranraer; Barty, Kirkcolm; Dougall, Stoneykirk; Gibson, Glenapp; Gellie, Leswalt; John M'Clew, Esq., Dinvin; Alex. Rankin, Esq., Aird; John Todd, Esq., Auchleach; John Gordon, Esq., Stranraer; Drs Orgill and Easton, Stranraer; W. M. Leslie, Esq., editor of the *Galloway Gazette;* Messrs Gibb and Bisset, Stranraer; Kennedy, South Cairn; Cumming, Kirkcolm, &c.—being a representation of all the Presbyterian Churches of Scotland.

On the motion of Dr ORGILL, Mr Stewart, yr. of Southwick, was called to the chair. The Rev. Mr DOUGALL, Stoneykirk, opened the meeting with prayer.

The CHAIRMAN, who was received with applause, said—Before commencing the formal part of this evening's proceedings I hope I may be allowed in your name to give a hearty and cordial welcome to those gentlemen—strangers to many of us—who have come so far, and put themselves to so much inconvenience, to be present with us to-night. I have only to mention the names of Dr Begg, Mr Kidston of Ferniegair, and the Rev. Mr Turnbull, to elicit a warm greeting from you. I shall also read some letters from others who, though absent in body, are present in spirit with us, and who desire to express their sympathy and approval of the object of our meeting. Lord Dalrymple writes:—"With regard to the educational meeting to be held in Stranraer on the 24th instant, which I regret extremely being unable to attend, but beg to express my sympathy with all the objects of the meeting, and hope that, in particular, the endeavours to retain the Bible in the schools may meet with success." Sir John D. Hay, Bart., writes:—"I cordially concur in the resolutions, and only regret that the short notice, and other engagements which press on me so soon before the meeting of Parliament, make it impracticable for me to come down and support you. I hope and pray that not only from your meeting, but from all Scotland, a voice will arise which will speak in terms which must be listened to, insisting that Scotland is a Christian nation, which is determined to manage the education of her children for herself; that the true foundation of all Christian teaching is the Bible; and that those who teach shall be equitably remunerated and fitly trained." Colonel M'Douall of Logan, writes:—"I regret my health will not admit of my being present at the meeting on the Education Bill to-morrow. I assure you I sympathise most cordially with the movement, and consider the attempt of the Lord Advocate and the Government to revolutionise and secularise the whole system of our Scottish education, preventing the Word of God being taught and read in our schools, a disgrace to any Christian country. I hope you will have a successful meeting." Mr Charles Kerr of Larbrax writes:—" I most heartily agree with the speakers on the subject they are taking up. It is a disgrace to the ministers and people of Scotland if they do not do everything in their power against the proposed system of secular teaching, without the religious teaching along with it." Mr William Martin of Larbrax also writes:— " I sympathise very much with the objects of the meeting, and would have gladly availed myself of the honour and privilege of giving countenance and support to such a noble and worthy cause had not a prior engagement," &c. Sir William Wallace, Bart., Robert Johnston Stewart of Physgill, and others, have signified their approval and sympathies with the meeting— (applause). For myself, although I feel it is a great honour to take part in the meeting as your Chairman, I cannot under-rate the responsibility of my office. While I see around me many far more able than myself, I feel unwilling to take advantage of the privilege of the chair, yet, while cheerfully yielding the palm of advocacy, I shall not give way to any one in the interest I feel in this great question. The objects of this meeting are exceedingly simple and intelligible. They are to secure to Scotland a religious education, sanctioned by the Legislature; the entire control and management of our schools; and the right remuneration and training of those who carry on their administration. We find this met by a Bill hostile to the resolutions of which we are about to ask your approval, and of that Bill I now speak. The present Government has given us two Education Bills. The Bill of 1869 contained somewhat similar provisions to the one proposed to be brought in this coming session. Against some of those I petitioned along with others, and I may say our petition was granted, as considerable modification was made in the House of Lords where the Bill was first brought in. We did not petition against it as a whole, not wishing to impede legislation on the subject, but on the same points as are brought before you to-night. I mention this to show that this is not the first session I have taken an interest in this question. Nor am I hostile to the whole Bill. In 1871, practically the same Bill was introduced. With reference to it, 1059 petitions were lodged—98 were against it, and 909 for amendments, signed by 76,444 persons, while only 52 were for it, signed by 4868 persons. The voice of Scotland was raised against it, and a great part of her intellect and intelligence. We expected something different from the Government after so decided an expression of opinion. At last the oracle has spoken, and true to the utterances of all oracles, it has made us little wiser than before, unless to inform us that the Bill is to remain almost unchanged. Let us then consider some of the points we have to take up to-night. I find it is the rule that, if you give a just and proper remuneration, men will work better, and show more anxiety in the discharge of their work. This is the case in the three northern counties, where, owing to the munificence of one individual, the schoolmasters have larger salaries than in the other parts of Scotland, and turn out better scholars. I find nothing in the Bill to warrant us in supposing that they will be soon as well off as at present. It is the glory of this country that her sons do well, and should continue to do well in the world. I have travelled much in my days, and whether in the far north of Canada, or in the western prairies of America, or in the sultry east, we find the Scotchman first in the path of progress. He has a steadiness and trustworthiness which gives him character, and that is his success, and the groundwork of that character is his Bible teachings—(applause). But the Lord Advocate sneers at our Parochial Schools, and sneers at our clergy as well. He says,—" All the religion of the country is not concentrated in the parish minister," and that the Parish Schools do not turn out the same class of scholars as formerly. He tells us one in 400 now learn Latin, and one in 500 Greek, and the odd 25 out of 10,825 go now to a university. I do not think it would be a great advantage, or any advantage if every ploughman's son learned Latin, but I like a poor man to be able to give his son, if that son prove capable of receiving such instruction, a first-class education, that he may rise and help himself hereafter; and if our education is not so first-class as formerly, that is the fault of the London Board, and that is the reason we require the control of our own education —(applause). Consider for a moment our past legislation : 175

years ago England and Scotland started on an equal footing in education—one was rich and opulent, and the other poor—the one had a voluntary system, the other, Scotland, a system fenced by legislative enactments. Now the first is last, and the last is first—(applause). Not so long ago the Privy Council decreed that every school must be connected with a church, in order to obtain Privy Council inspection and grants; and also that the inspector of the school should be a member of the church with which the school was connected. Twenty years afterwards the revised code ordained that the schools assisted must be connected with a recognised religious denomination, that the Scriptures of the authorised version should be daily read, and that the Committee of Council should consult the religious and educational bodies before appointing inspectors. That was all very well, but it has not been carried out; and now, although it is the duty of inspectors to examine in religion, they rarely *report* upon it, and practically are not required to do so; so religious teaching is less attended to, and because the greater importance is attached to the three R's the higher branches are discouraged—(applause). The case was very different in the times of our forefathers. In the First Book of Discipline, laid before the Great Council for Scotland—which was, I believe, the first General Assembly— by John Knox, in 1560, he says, " It is of necessity that your honours be most careful for the virtuous education and godly upbringing of the youth of this realm, if either ye now thirst unfainedly the advancement of Christ's glorie, or yet desire the continuance of his benefits to the generation following." This " godly upbringing of the young" he speaks of, I need hardly tell you, is *Bible teaching*. But we are told up to this time no Acts of Parliament enact religion to be taught in our schools. At all events they do not discourage it, as this Bill does, and they *do* secure it by legislative authority. In 1567 an old Act speaks of " loss to souls of the young if God's Word be not rooted in them." In 1696 our Parochial Schools were established, and, practically, religion with them. In the Act of 1803 it is enacted " that the superintendence of schools shall continue with the ministers of the Established Church," and further, that Presbyteries are to regulate the hours of teaching, &c., and that the schoolmaster is required to conform to and obey all regulations so made by the Presbytery. In 1861 a religious test was applied to schoolmasters. All this time religion was uppermost. If you say there was no special enactment, it was because none was required; it was as much the duty of the schoolmaster to teach religion as anything else in the school, and he was supervised by the minister of the parish. And in this critical time in Scotland's history we have more need of religion than ever. Secularism is abroad, and that school of men tell us religion will still be taught; but we want a legislative enactment and guarantee—(applause). The last decree of the Birmingham Education League was, "that no permission to teach religion be granted." Oh, but that is England, you say; no, but Scotland was represented from the secularists, and the Rev. Robert Craig says, "In national schools nothing should be taught requiring a conscience clause." That surely means no religion at any price—(applause). What did a Cabinet Minister, Mr Lowe, say at Halifax the other day—"When they paid for secular results, and gave no payment for religious instruction, this tended greatly to secularise the religious instruction in these schools." He claimed that as a great merit and benefit, though it had been much complained of. We could manage our poor boards by a Board of Supervision. Why not equally our schools?—(applause). This Bill ignores religion entirely—limits it to the narrowest amount, and puts obstructions in its way, as, for example, in having "a time-table clause," which Lord Shaftesbury declares will give us "the least possible religious instruction." To all intents, our teaching has been increasingly secular for years. You are now asked to make it professedly and completely secular. But you say there are difficulties. What! with 96 per cent of our population Protestants, and 4 Roman Catholics! Or 85 per cent Presbyterians. But the local boards, we are told, will give us religious teaching as heretofore. Well, last year in London I attended the meetings of the London School Board—some 40 of the ablest men London could produce. They spent days, and weeks, and months in discussing whether the Bible should be taught or not; at last it was resolved it should be just such instruction thereupon as was suited to the capacity of children, but no catechism or formulary should be used. Why should not all this wrangling take place again at the end of three years?—(applause). But if Imperial Parliament settled the question once for all, it would probably rest, and not be re-opened in three years; and our local boards would see their way to carry it out—(applause). I do not believe many parents would object to have their children taught religion. Many of them find no time to teach the Bible, others fail in ability. It appears, the Lord Advocate considers that, because the teaching of religion is not eminently satisfactory, we should put ourselves in the position in which possibly we might have none at all. What an argument to use!—(applause). I do not understand the Voluntaries; apparently they are willing to accept the local boards, but refuse to pay for religion. Why, if they pay the rate assessed by the boards, and these boards teach religion, they still pay for religion. Whether the rate comes directly from their own pocket, or indirectly from the same source, but through the Government, in principle it is the same. If it is wrong to receive money from the State for religious teaching, it must be equally wrong to receive it from the rates. Both must equally offend the conscience, so no religion will be taught at all by the schoolmaster in receipt of his ordinary salary. But if religion is insisted upon in the school, then there must be a religious voluntary rate for those who wish to have religion taught. How would you like that?—(hear). The Irish difficulty seems to stagger most people: Because I am to have my Bible taught my child, the Irishman is to have his Bible taught his child; but if I am to go without my Bible, then the Irishman is to go without his Bible, which he will refuse to do, judging from the last manifesto of Cardinal Cullen. As the Roman Catholics will not be guided by what we do here, so we need not be ruled by what is done there—(applause). But, after all, this is an experiment, you may say, and it may succeed. I reply, it has never yet succeeded. In 1865 I went to America to judge the question for myself there. You have a local rate and local boards, and secular instruction. I may say it was partly to obtain this very information that I went there. At Boston, the great educational centre, I had the best introductions, and the best opportunities. I found the schools in secular education excellent. I examined both the elementary and high class schools. I asked the Chief Superintendent of the State Education Department—Is the Bible regularly read? "Well, sir," he said, "that is our constitution (if agreeable to the ratepayers), and for some years we carried it out, but a few Roman Catholic priests objected, so, although we had it tried in a court of law, and gained our lawsuit"—note this, "for peace sake, and the impossibility of agreement, we have given it up." That was the purport of his answer, and that is what may occur here—(applause). The effect there is, that a large number of parents are withdrawing their children from the rate-school, and sending them to those in which religion is taught. They are thus establishing a system of denominational schools, although they already pay so high a rate to the State schools. They say they want a school between the family and the Church. In Germany, it is an essential feature of education that the people *will* have religion taught in the elementary schools. It is considered the most important element. The different States have tried the secular, the mixed, the denominational schools, and have now adopted the latter system, which, the Report of the Royal Commission on Education tells us, also supplies the education of Scotland, in her Established and Free Church schools. Prussia has gone through the very experiment we are asked to try, and finds it unsuitable to the real wants of the people. In Holland there is a growing dissatisfaction with the Government system, because no religion is taught, and the Government schools are consequently being neglected. In France, by the Code Napoleon, and M. Guizot's law of 1833, the secular system was established in every commune. I need not remind you of the sad decline of religion in France, where the goddess Reason has been worshipped, and morality and virtue disregarded. Father Hyacinthe tells us :—" The first wound, which we may call that of the right hand—the hand that carries the light—is the darkening of the Word of God "—(applause). In conclusion, I shall only say, we believe the kingdom of Great Britain and Ireland to be a Protestant kingdom. The gospel of Jesus Christ, diffused through its laws, sustaining its throne, spread among the people, taught to its youth, is still the preserving salt of the kingdom, and we mean it shall continue so—(applause). I should like to take a plebiscite on the subject. The very heathen taught their children religion. May we not teach the designs of Providence through the instrumentality of nations like Babylon, Persia, or Rome. Scotland, in accepting this Bill, will sin against great light and great experience. Let us increase the quantity of our education, and not deteriorate from the quality. Enlarge the constitution of your schools, associate all Protestant ministers on your board. The spirit of rivalry will die out, animosity and misgivings will fade away, when all sects are united under the old banner of " use and wont," to teach the religion of Jesus Christ—(applause). Let us hold many meetings like this, if necessary, to support our cause, for

> " From scenes like these old Scotia's grandeur springs,
> That makes her loved at home, revered abroad."

—(loud applause).

The Rev. W. B. TURNBULL of Townhead Parish, Glasgow, moved the first resolution,—"That it is essential to any system of national education for Scotland that it recognise and make due provision for the religious instruction of the young in public schools." After a few introductory remarks on the importance of the subject, he said,—In trying to persuade this large and influential meeting to adopt this resolution, it would be worse than useless for me to try to conceal the fact that I stand here to-night, not so much with the view of propounding that which is new, as honestly and faithfully to declare and defend that which I believe to be true—(hear, hear). The importance of the subject which we are here to discuss has been conceded on all hands. However much we may differ in our views in regard to what are the best means for educating the people of this country, we are all agreed as to the absolute necessity of securing as speedily as possible some means by which the educational wants of the country may be supplied; and therefore I wish it to be understood that we are here to-night, not as the enemies but as the friends of national education—(applause). But we are here, sir, as the uncompromising enemies of any effort being made to withdraw the Bible from the public schools of this country, and thereby heap reproach on the memory of our patriotic forefathers, who, to secure which, suffered both persecution and death; and we are encouraged to persevere in our present movement in the belief that the principles with which we are identified are held by the vast majority of our fellow-countrymen; for I have no hesitation in saying that so far as I have been able to ascertain, the national feeling on this question, as expressed in our daily newspapers (which must be regarded as the exponents of public opinion), that feeling must be acknowledged as favourable to religious instruction in our public schools, and therefore I regard it as a self-evident proposition, that any system of education, to be truly national, must be religious in its character. I cannot help saying, sir, that it would be strange, after all that this country has done and suffered in defence of Bible truth, if any other feeling than that prevailed—(hear, hear). The subject which has brought together so many individuals in this large hall to-night is one intimately connected with our individual and national prosperity; for I take leave to say that no question can be personally more important than the religious question,—for this simple reason, that religion is not a matter of expediency or inexpediency, but is essentially bound up with our temporal and eternal interests. No question can be more important politically,—for this very reason, that religion has for the last three centuries been pre-eminently the moving-spring of our national and political life work. If then, sir, the question is confessedly of so vast importance, it becomes us surely to view it seriously, impartially, and with as little as possible of religious bigotry or party political fanaticism—(Cheers). If I have been able to form a right opinion on this question there are at present four different theories before the people of this country, each of which has its sympathisers and supporters. There is first of all the denominational system, in which it is proposed to put all the religious denominations of this country on terms of perfect equality. Then there is what is called the " use and wont " system, by which it is proposed to maintain our parochial schools, extended and resuscitated; thirdly, we have the theory entertained by those parties who propose to give us the maximum of secular with the minimum of religious instruction, in order, as they say, to avoid sectarian controversies; and lastly, we have the theory of the Lord Advocate, as propounded from this very platform on the 4th of this month, and which he told you would be embodied in the Bill which he hoped to introduce in the ensuing session of Parliament, by which religious teaching would, in his opinion, be neither *prescribed* nor *proscribed*, but left to the control of local boards in various parts of the country. I have said, sir, that there are four educational theories at this moment before the country, and that the question is, Which of these theories is the best, and consequently ought to receive our sympathy and support? Now, while it is true that nominally there are FOUR, it is equally true that there are in reality only TWO. The denominational theory and the "use and wont" are but different phases of the religious question; while, on the other hand, the third-mentioned theory and that of the Lord Advocate are, as I shall try to prove, but attempts to introduce by covert means a system of unlimited secularism—(loud cheers). Why, sir, in the very nature of the case there can only be two. The one religious, the other, though designated unsectarian, is, when closely examined, nothing short of a non-religious theory—(hear). Hence, the question to be decided by us is, Religion, or No religion—(applause); for in the present state of this country it is impossible to introduce even the most elementary religious truths without jarring with the religious or irreligious prejudices of some portion of the community. This, sir, is a difficulty which even the Lord Advocate and his supporters have confessed to be great—a difficulty, moreover, which they have endeavoured to meet, but in their effort to meet it they have in my opinion made a most miserable failure. By this THIRD theory it is proposed, you will observe, to give to the people of this country *religious instruction*, but not *instruction in religion*. Now, let us mark the distinction! While if by the teaching of religion is meant the inculcating of those doctrines which are peculiar to revealed religion, we are to understand by a religious teaching on the other hand, to use the language of the Lord Advocate, "That a certain piety shall accompany all the efforts of the schoolmaster in teaching the young; that he shall use all legitimate occasions to instruct the mind and the heart of a child in those things not involving any doctrinal questions at all, or any teaching of religion in that sense which gives occasion to controversy." Now, sir, what I would ask you to observe is this, that in the present state of society such a union of secular and religious instruction as that is simply impossible—(hear). The *banns* may be proclaimed, and certainly have been loudly proclaimed of late by the advocates of this theory; but let them dare *to celebrate the marriage*, and I venture to affirm that many parties will be found ready to object. Now, sir, do not misunderstand me. What I affirm is not that you cannot unite secular and religious instruction to secure, if possible, such a union in the forthcoming Bill. I am here to-night, and we have a right, to demand it, from the fact that the existence of such a union has, for nearly 300 years, been the glory of this country—(cheers). But what I assert is this, that it is impossible, in the present condition of society, even to refer to religion without, in some way, jarring with the predilections of some; and hence, that you have no alternative between a voluntary liberal system and a purely secular system—(hear, hear). Having illustrated this view of the question, Mr Turnbull continued—What truth, for example, could be more elementary than the existence of God? And yet it must be known to you all that, should a teacher inculcate even that self-evident proposition, there are infidels and materialists in this country prepared to protest, on the ground that such teaching is sectarian—(hear). Or, again, let the teacher go but one step further, and assert that we have a common Father in God, and that, consequently, humanity is a universal brotherhood, and is it not apparent that these Deists and Pantheists may raise the hue and cry of sectarianism being taught in our national rate-paid schools? Why, sir, I would go further, and say, that if such a system of education be introduced, then no teacher must presume to begin his daily duties by a form of devotion, or by supplicating the blessing of Almighty God—(hear)—for are there not those in this country who, misled by science, falsely so-called, have reached the unenviable position of esteeming prayer insanity, or unmitigated superstition?—(applause). Therefore I maintain that, as society is at present constituted, we may have religious or secular; but if secular, then we must become entirely non-religious, and if religious, then in some sense, and to some extent, denominational in its merit, though, as has been shown in Scotland, not denominational in reality. There are these two alternatives, and there is no third. One or other of these we must accept, and should we say "religion," then we must be prepared to brave this cry of sectarianism, which will undoubtedly be raised by infidels and Deists. But should we say (which God forbid) secular, then "Ichabod" may be written on the revered walls of Britain's institutions; for I maintain that we can only have it at the expense of being without God, and without religious instruction for our children—(loud cheers). I have already said, sir, that the Lord

Advocate's theory is very much akin to that which I have been attempting to review. But I now add, with this difference, that his theory is decidedly the worst, inasmuch as, by his Bill, no religious teaching whatever is to be given in any school, unless otherwise provided by the local boards, while he at the same time has taken care so to frame his Bill as to encourage both the boards and the teachers to exclude religious teaching. The teacher is to receive no allowances for giving religious instruction, and therefore cannot be expected to give it. The inspector is not to examine the pupils on religious subjects, but he is to examine them on secular subjects, for which parliamentary grants are to be given, in which grants the teacher is to participate according to the way in which his pupils pass the examination on these secular subjects, so that his self-interest is appealed to in favour of his whole time being devoted to secular teaching, to the exclusion of religious instruction—(hear). Again, granting that, in some cases, these proposed local boards should express a wish to have religious instruction in the school, the question arises, Will those teachers who are to succeed our parochial schoolmasters be qualified to impart it? On this point I would have you to observe that those men are to be trained as teachers in Normal Seminaries, in which, of course, like the public schools, religion is to have no definite footing. Thus, you will perceive, that these young men, in preparing themselves for the duties of teachers, will require to spend the two years previous to their entering upon duty in a seminary where no religion can be inculcated. Will that, sir, be a likely training for preparing teachers to take charge of the children of this country? or will these men be qualified to impart that religious instruction which some local boards may desire? I emphatically answer that they will not. And thus, sir, I am forced to the conclusion that the whole scope and tendency of the proposed Bill will be to drive religious instruction out of our public schools; and this has been the aim of men occupying, at this moment, high positions in the Government of this country. For example, the Chancellor of the Exchequer, the other day at Halifax, when speaking of the Government delegating its duty, not to persons chosen by themselves, but to any number of persons who came forward to found schools, said—"That system I was never weary of denouncing; but I am sorry to say, that in so denouncing it, I met with very little or any support in Parliament; and not being able otherwise to reform the system in connection with my colleague, Lord Granville, I hit on the scheme of paying by results, which had a peculiar value of its own, because it tended to insure a sufficient quantity of work for the money paid for it. But it had another and further advantage. By paying for secular results, and giving no payment at all for religious instruction, we adopted a system tending very forcibly to the secularisation of education "—(hear, hear). Thus the right honourable gentleman introduces the revised code for the express purpose, on his own confession, of excluding religious instruction from the schools of this country—(loud cheers). He uses his influence as a statesman, and the public money, in order to bring about, by *stratagem*, what he was *unable* to accomplish by *fair means*, for want of support in Parliament from the people's representatives. And thus I am forced to the conclusion that, while we should insist on Government putting religious instruction on the same footing as that of secular teaching, there must also be some force organised by the people themselves, so as to prevent our public men from adopting a policy so destructive to the best interests of the nation—(cheers)—for if there be any question in which the people of this country are deeply interested that question is the one which we are here this evening to promote, and that for reasons apart altogether from its religious aspect—for it is well known that, to a very large extent, schools have been erected throughout the country by large donations from wealthy and benevolent men. Why, sir, the Royal Commissioners on Education declare that the supplementary system of schools, supplied by voluntary effort, "furnishes more than two-thirds of the education of the rural districts of Scotland, and on which that of the towns mainly depends "—(hear). It is brought out in their report that, while the number of parochial, side, and parliamentary schools was only 1133, with a roll of 88,183 scholars, the number of schools supplied by voluntary effort was 3318, with a roll of 224,612 scholars. In connection with my own church in the city of Glasgow, we are at present erecting a school, in a missionary locality, at a cost of nearly £5000, all done on the voluntary principle—(hear, hear). But the tendency of the proposed Bill will be to bring all such good work to an end—to dry up the streams of philanthropy, at the expense of increasing the taxation of the country, in which all classes, but especially working men, are deeply interested—(applause). And what is all this for? To " put an end to all denominational teaching and sectarian strife," is the reply which is made by the advocates of this secular system. Why, sir, there has been no denominational teaching in our public schools: children connected with all religious denominations have been found, and are still found, and no charge has ever been brought forward of any attempt being made to proselytise them from the faith of their fathers; nay, but all the strife has been confined to a few political agitators and ecclesiastical partizans, who, in the name of toleration, wish to oppose and put down all who differ from themselves—(loud cheers)—and yet, forsooth, these are the men at whose shrine the Lord Advocate for Scotland bows in humble submission—(hear, hear). And, therefore, I stand here and ask you to join with me in lodging our public protest against his proposed Bill, inasmuch as it utterly fails to meet the educational wants of the country,—in the language of Professor Smeaton of Edinburgh, " the country has asked bread, and he has given it a stone." No one deplores more than I do, the condition of the thousands in our land who are living in ignorance. No one could be more willing than I am to accept of any system of education which would at all cope with the social difficulties of our country, or secure the amelioration of the lapsed masses in our midst. But I fail to see, sir, that secular education is that long wished-for philosopher's stone which is to transmute all our brazen woes into golden weals—(hear). Nay, I am every day the more convinced that no system of education, which is not religious, can meet the wants of society, or supply the defects in our present parochial system—(loud cheers). Labouring as I am every day in a district inhabited by many who are both poor and degraded, I know the difficulty of inducing the children to attend the *Sabbath school;* and unless some means be adopted to secure their attendance at the *day school,* and, when there, to instruct them in the truths of the Gospel, they will grow up pests to society, and dangerous to the State—(hear, hear). What we require, sir, is not less religion, but more. We can indeed afford to dispense with much of our religious bigotry, and party ecclesiastical zeal. But there is one thing common to us all, and dear to us all, with which we cannot, and dare not dispense, and that is the glorious Gospel of God. As Christian men, who have felt the saving power of religion, we desire to secure it for our countrymen ; and as Christian parents, we have a right to demand it for our children ; and because the Lord Advocate's Bill seeks to rob us of that right, I call upon you as men, as parents, and as Christians, to seize the trumpet of an enlightened public opinion, and blow a blast which will consign it to the grave of everlasting oblivion—(loud and prolonged applause).

The REV. T. BARTY said—Although I have been happily relieved from the responsibility of proposing the first motion, by the presence of my friend Mr Turnbull, I must ask your indulgence while I offer you some further observations on the subject of this resolution, even though I should be but " twice slaying the slain." Believing that we are now passing through an important crisis in the history of this country, and that a serious danger threatens our educational institutions, I consider it an urgent duty to use every effort towards preserving our present system in its essential and characteristic features. I have pleasure in addressing this magnificent audience convened in the burgh of Stranraer, and the more so that it reminds me of a meeting which was held here last year in connection with the Education Bill which has happily been withdrawn. I remember that when I was called upon at that meeting to propose the first of a series of resolutions which at the time attained some notoriety, I found the views which are to be advocated here this evening were most cordially endorsed by the large majority of a meeting, of whose cordiality I was at first by no means well assured. That meeting proved, in the most significant manner, that in this town and neighbourhood there existed a deep-seated and wide-spread opposition to the leading principles of the abortive Bill of last Session— (cheers). The mention of last year's meeting reminds me that we miss to-night the well-remembered features* of one who then eloquently pleaded the cause in support of which I now address you, but who has since then sunk into an early grave, lamented by many who now hear me. Since the conflict in which we are now engaged commenced, many good men and true to whom the cause was dear, have fallen from the ranks, and are now "where, beyond these voices there is peace." The more need that we who remain should with strong hand hold aloft the banner under which they were marshalled— the banner which has been consecrated by our fathers' prayers, yea, by our fathers' blood, and which we trust will yet wave untarnished over the land that is dear to us, and the children whom we love—to them, as it has been to us, a glory and a defence !—(prolonged cheering). The remarkable speech which was lately delivered in this hall, and of which I have one or two things to say before I sit down, compels me to remember that I appear before you as a parish minister. Indeed I claim to be heard as a minister of the Church of Scotland to whom the educational interests of my parish have been and are matter of the supremest interest, and which I have ever done my best to promote—(cheers). I dislike to speak in this personal vein, but I believe I have your sympathy, and there are times where self-vindication is justifiable, and even necessary. And I take it upon me to say, that the parish ministers of Scotland have, on the whole, faithfully and zealously discharged their duties in this department—(cheers). Now, sir, I must repel the insinuation which has been thrown at me more than once, that under cover of a zeal for religious instruction I am agitating merely to retain my position

* The late Rev. John M'Calman.

(which seems in some quarters an object of envy) as *ex officio* manager of the parish school. If that were my purpose, I should not be found on the same platform with Dr Begg and Mr Kidston—(cheers). And for my part I do not see how, in any national system which shall absorb the Free Church schools and others, the parish minister could be continued as the only *ex officio* member of the board. But if it should be necessary to sever the connection that has hitherto subsisted between the parish minister and the parish school, it might not be unbecoming a great and magnanimous Government, in effecting the separation, to make some acknowledgment of past services, and to admit, what cannot be denied, that ever since 1696 parish ministers have done as much as any class of the community to promote the cause of Scottish education —(applause). This has been fully admitted and amply proved by the various reports of the Commissioners and Assistant Commissioners to the House of Commons. The right honourable gentleman may find it needful to deprive me of my present position in the parish school, but I naturally object to allow myself to be kicked out at the door, even though the sight might be welcome to some people. If Mr Young had any deliberate intention to hold up the parochial clergy to derision, I think he acted unworthily and ungenerously, and that he has not gained thereby the sympathy of the great mass of the Scottish people, or of the heritors of the land. I believe that when the day comes that the heritor's board holds its last meeting in connection with the parish school, the heritors and the ministers of Scotland will part with mutual feelings of kindness and respect—(cheers). I regret that I am obliged to take up your time with some observations on the Lord Advocate's speech to his constituents, especially in its relations to the resolution now before you. Having bestowed some attention on a speech so interesting and important to Scotland, I have been struck with the unusual effusiveness which it displays. It is much more "gushing" and sentimental than might have been expected. To explain this characteristic I have hit upon a geographical theory. The learned gentleman's periodical visits to this remote corner of the West has brought him within the reach of Irish influences, and accordingly we find in his speech a not very faint suspicion of what over the water is called "blarney"—(laughter and cheers). Or to put my criticism in an Irish form, "If it had not been his Lordship that was speaking, I should have said he was trying to throw dust in people's eyes"—(applause). I believe Mr Young would not have so spoken if

B

he had felt his position to be a strong one, and he was honest enough to let out that a great portion of what he said had no meaning in particular, inasmuch as notwithstanding all the sentiment and blarney, the Bill is to be the same as before! Now, sir, the style of rhetoric in which the learned gentleman indulged on the occasion of his recent visit has some obvious advantages in addressing a popular assembly; but it has also serious drawbacks. It is apt to be incorrect as to fact, and halting in argument; and I propose, with your permission, to show that, with respect to the momentous question of religious instruction, he was singularly inconsequential and inaccurate. Take one or two specimens of the kind of logic which, without any unfair or forced construction, may be gathered from his Lordship's words. "Religious instruction is of the first importance religiously, educationally, and politically; and without religious instruction, a child is not educated even elementarily in such a manner as to fit him for his duties in the world, in any station, however humble." But "religious instruction, at present, is given most unsatisfactorily at most parish schools," therefore, "in my Education Bill I shall not prescribe any religious instruction." By his own admission, he does not propose to provide for the children of Scotland such an education as will fit them for their duties in the world. This is his own account of the coming Bill. Again, "the people of Scotland are a very religious people;" but "they are leaving 90,000 children to grow up in ignorance and sin, and require to be compelled to send their children to school." Therefore, "the people of Scotland may well be trusted to provide religious instruction for all the children of the nation." Again, "the people of Scotland are 86 per cent Presbyterians, agreed that religion shall be taught, and what religion shall be taught;" but "the people of Scotland are hopelessly divided about religion, they will never be able to settle their controversies, and their divisions are keeping 90,000 children in ignorance and vice." Therefore, "in my Bill I shall not say what religion shall be taught, I shall not even venture to say that any religion shall be taught at all, but I shall throw the religious question to be fought over in local boards, in which divisions will be intensified and embittered by being confined in narrower space." Doubtless, our religious divisions have done grievous harm, and have hindered our progress in education. But perhaps abortive legislation has quite as much retarded us; and it deserves to be remembered that our divisions have at least created the important supplement of the Free Church schools—(cheers).

Mr Young refers in a cursory manner to the three plans suggested as to religious instruction. He at once condemns the " denominational," and yet has a denominational clause in his Bill. He says the " use and wont " system is impossible. Let us remind him that it now exists. Let us demand that it be continued! He does not conceal his own preference for the "secular" system, but is not honest and manly enough to give effect to his own principles. Sir, I wish that he had given us a secular Bill—a Bill, that is, which is avowedly secular, and the true character of which could not be hidden by any sophistry or quibbling. Then, I think we should have had upon our side some of our friends who, a few years ago, were entirely with us, but who now can only hope, and deprecate, and doubt whether they are empowered to protest, and are mainly anxious not in any way to hinder the Government from passing a Bill—(hear, hear, cheers, and applause). But not only are Mr Young's statements regarding the religious question exceedingly illogical, they are also at variance with fact. He is reported to have said at Wigtown, that " in respect to religious instruction he did not propose to make any change whatever; on that point there was no legal provision in Scotland, and there never had been." In making such an extraordinary and unfounded assertion he was either ignorant or disingenuous. I should be sorry to say that he was concealing what he knew regarding the present law of Scotland, but it is not very comforting to be forced to the conclusion that he is proposing to revolutionise our parochial system without being aware of its present condition and distinguishing characteristics—(hear, and prolonged cheering). The earliest Scotch Acts respecting education thus describe the great object which they had in view. It was " to exercise and train the youth in civilitie, godliness, knowledge, and learning—to bring them up in the fear of God, and that God's Word be rooted in them." And by the present law of Scotland, all teachers of parochial schools, and of schools established in terms of Act 1st and 2d Vict., chap. 87, are bound by a solemn declaration " faithfully to conform in their teaching to the doctrines of the Shorter Catechism "—(cheers). I should like to know, sir, if any legislative provision could be more express and binding? Then, in all those schools connected with the Church of Scotland, in all the Free Church Schools, and in many others besides,—in fact, in the vast majority of the schools which have been raised to supplement the parochial system,—there exists in their constitution deeds, feu-charters, and other legal instruments, the most strict provision for the maintenance of religious teaching—(cheers). I may instance those schools in this district which are supported by the Fergusson Trustees, who, under the provisions of the Lord Advocate's Bill, will be prevented from continuing these grants—(hear, hear, and prolonged applause). Now, sir, all the securities which at present exist in Acts of Parliament, constitutions of churches, and deeds of schools, are to be swept away, and the religious training of the young, which we have hitherto believed to require all this protection and encouragement, and more if it could have been got, is to be thrown into the hands of ratepayers' boards, who by this Bill are not to receive any distinct authority to take action in the matter, and who are in every way to be hindered from doing what is assumed they will all be most anxious to do!—(applause). And what are the arguments or inducements by which we are tempted to accede to this great educational revolution? First of all, we are to be bribed. We are to get a large grant from Government, and the heritors of Scotland are to be relieved from their present burdens. I hope, sir, that with all our mercenary proclivities, we are not thus to be seduced —(cheers). Then we are asked to consent to the overthrow of our school system in deference to the tender consciences of our fellow-countrymen who are opposed upon principle to the national recognition of religion in a national system of education, either because they disapprove of religious teaching altogether, or because they think it sinful to apply public money to the payment of religious teaching. It is chiefly in the interests of the so-called Voluntary party that the inducement I refer to is urged. And what is Voluntaryism? Let us hear the true account of this principle from Mr Renton of Kelso, one of its ablest and most consistent exponents :—" The principle on which I have always stood in this question, is the one laid down by the Church to which I belong, ' that it is not within the province of the State to provide for the religious instruction of the subject.' That principle excludes the provision by the State for religious instruction in schools, as well as in churches ; and it is not unreasonable to observe that it was in relation to the former that the United Presbyterian Synod first, and has often since, deliberately and unanimously enunciated it. What the Parliament may not enact it may not delegate to another and inferior body to enact with its authority. But this it would do if, declining to regulate the religious instruction to be given in schools, it empowered the local board of each locality to do so—(cheers). These local boards are not religious, still less Voluntary bodies. They are purely civil bodies, created by statute, having no powers but what statute gives them, and possessing the authority of the State to enforce them." This is, no doubt, the view which all Voluntaries who understand, and are true to their principles, are compelled to take of the matter in question. And now, let me call your attention to a very important statement made by the Lord Advocate at Stranraer, in answer to a question. He said—"The payment of the master for religious instruction must be in the salary which he receives, and the fees which the pupils pay." If it be the case, then, that under the proposed Bill, school boards may pay the teacher out of the rates for teaching religion, and authorise him to exact fees for the same, we are clearly warranted to maintain this alternative proposition, which I would respectfully submit to the candid consideration of our Voluntary friends, either the Lord Advocate's Bill is utterly opposed to their principles, and cannot be accepted or implemented by them, or they can reconcile it with their consciences to pay for religious teaching out of public rates—(cheers). But if they can do that and still be Voluntaries, they might have put their scruples in their pockets, and joined with us in demanding "use and wont," and still be Voluntaries after all!—(great cheering). But, sir, we are besought, in the interests of Protestantism, to accept the proposals of the right honourable gentleman. This argument, I think, might have been suggested by Cardinal Cullen himself—(laughter). Let me ask how will this Bill affect the Roman Catholics of Scotland. I rather fancy that they will not find it necessary to oppose it very strenuously! They are to see the Bible ejected from the Protestant schools of Scotland, and are to be permitted to have their own denominational schools, wherever they are strong enough to demand them, wherever such schools "are specially needed." But we are told to consider the case of Ireland. Well, sir, I wish that the Protestants of Scotland were as likely to get their own way as the Papists of Ireland! But if such a Bill as this were enacted for Ireland, I am much at a loss to see in what special way Protestantism would be a gainer—(hear, hear, and cheers). In the great majority of cases the local boards would be composed of Papists, who would have the power of applying the rates to pay for the teaching of their religion. We are asked to do evil to Scotland that good may come to Ireland! But what suppose the Irish people will not accept the good? How foolish and infatuated shall we be, if, for a very hypothetical benefit to Ireland, we surrender a very certain and precious benefit to ourselves !—(hear, hear, and applause). And now, sir, I have only time to refer to the Time-table Clause. The Lord Advocate apparently disapproves of this clause, and if we could be certain that he would act upon his own convictions, we should be safe from such a detestable invention. But, meantime, it stands part of the second edition of last year's Bill—(hear, hear, and cheering). I believe, sir, it would be as well for the country to " proscribe " religious instruction in schools, as to have it under the restrictions of a time-table. One consequence of the time-table would be that all our school books must be revised or placed in an *index expurgatorius*—(applause). I am happy to say that our modern school books have on the whole a distinctly religious and Christian tone. But with a time-table, all the religious references they contain must be excised, or the whole of them thrown away. I could imagine such a scene as this taking place under the restriction of a time-table. A boy has been convicted of falsehood ; the teacher reproves him, and with solemn and kindly words reminds him of what the Holy Book of God says about liars. Whereupon the boy protests, " Sir, it's half-past ten ; I'll tell the managers !"—(laughter and applause). And the teacher would have to say, " I beg pardon, I should not have mentioned the Bible at this hour of the day, but remember I am authorised by the Lord Advocate for Scotland to tell you that " there is a God above you, spying out all your ways !"—(laughter and cheers). And this is the authority upon which our teachers are henceforth to be permitted during school hours to follow the dictates of " piety " in training the souls of the children committed to their care ! Let us resist with all our might such a travesty of religious teaching ; let us resist the threatened infringement of our privileges as the citizens of a Christian and Protestant State ; and, with the zeal and courage of a holy cause, let us call upon the British Parliament to maintain in all our schools that religious instruction which has been the " use and wont " of Scotland, and has made her great—(great cheering). And now, sir, I must have made a poor use of the time you have kindly allowed me if I have not shown reason why we should with all our heart adopt the motion which you are now to put from the chair—(the rev. gentleman resumed his seat amidst immense cheering).

Mr M‘Clew, Dinvin, supported the motion, and said he hoped meetings would be got up in all the parishes of Scotland against the Lord Advocate's Bill, for a worse Bill never could have been brought before Parliament. This was a Protestant nation, and they were degenerated very far if they accepted such a Bill. It seemed to him like sending a vessel to sea without compass or chart to send children to a school from which the Bible would be excluded. He would rather want their education altogether. He could not understand their Voluntary friends. There were 90,000 children in Glasgow without education, and as soon as they had got these taught it would show whether they could succeed or not— (applause.)

MR KIDSTON, of Ferniegair, rose and said—The motion which has been placed in my hands is as follows:—"That Scotland is entitled to retain in her own hands the management and control of her own schools, which have hitherto proved so great a blessing"—(cheers). I rejoice, sir, that I have an opportunity of standing forth before so large and intelligent an audience in defence of our time-honoured scriptural system of education on a public platform in the Rhins of Galloway—(hear). I observe that the Lord Advocate has been making a tour among his constituents here. But anything more unsatisfactory and contradictory than his statements on the education question can scarcely be imagined. He has been trying to throw a little dust in your eyes, I don't suppose with much success, but if by some mischance any has got in, it shall be our business to wipe it out to-night— (cheers and laughter). He says we may reasonably and confidently expect that the Scotch Education Bill will constitute the second measure of the Session. But, alas! his ears seem to have been closed to all that is stirring up Scotland, from one end of the land to the other. He makes a profession of great concern for religious instruction, saying that a child without knowledge is not educated, even elementarily, in such a manner as to fit him for his duties in the world, in any station, however humble—(hear)—and ends (oh, lame and impotent conclusion!) without making the slightest provision for such religious instruction. He told the meeting, from this platform on which I now have the privilege of standing, that the real authority will be found in the school boards. But how can that be when we take into account the unlimited control, of a secular kind only, exercised by the third code, framed in a "Star Chamber" in London, and that chamber consisting, as we know, of one star sitting on a three-legged stool—(cheers and laughter)—and when we consider also the control, check, and supervision of the so-called Scotch branch of the Privy Council in London, which two things take the management almost entirely out of the hands of the local boards? With these two blots in the arrangement, my audience will perceive at once where the real authority will lie. The Lord Advocate speaks again, with a kind of jaunty, saucy respect for the teacher, but makes not the slightest provision for his training, status, remuneration, or retiring allowance. We are told, in a misty and unsatisfactory manner, that religion, though not prescribed, is not to be proscribed. But even this, sir, is not correct, because religion is practically proscribed—first, by the proposed time-table; second, by the third code; and third, by placing the supreme control in a London board, which only professes to look at education from a secular point of view—(cheers). He speaks of the vast majority of the public of Scotland being in favour of religious instruction, and being, at the same time, agreed regarding the kind of religion to be taught—(hear, hear)— and candidly admits that in many places it will be absolutely impossible to have any instruction in the schools, except during school hours, and by the ordinary teacher. We are told by him that there was no law formerly for religious instruction. But, sir, our schools stood on the bold and conspicuous foundation, which was meant, not so much for instructing the children of the country in so many or so few branches of secular knowledge, but for the "godly upbringing of the young," by means of a national system of schools. No legislation has been introduced hitherto, of a nature to remove or even shake this foundation—(hear). Special legislation in favour of religious instruction was never wanted till the present moment; but now, with all the proposed overturn of our existing system, such legislation is urgently required. Let the Lord Advocate, if he is sincere, put an acknowledgment clause in the preamble of his Bill, to the effect that the fundamental principle of it is the "godly upbringing of the young"—(loud cheers). The great mass of feeling in Scotland under such a national system as is proposed, with a local board of very uncertain composition (even with the cumulative vote which we must insist should be tried in Scotland as it has been in England) is clearly in favour of some religion being legislatively required. At the very least, besides the acknowledgment in the preamble that it is not the intention of the Legislature to cancel or proscribe the "use and wont" of Scotland, we would require on this point a clause to the following effect:—" The branches of education, including religious instruction, according to 'use and wont,' shall be left to the determination of the local boards; provided always that the Holy Scriptures shall continue to be used in the schools as heretofore." We would require also the Inspector's clause recommended by the Royal Commission, which appeared in the Bill of 1869, to the effect of enabling the boards to insist that the Government Inspectors shall examine in religious knowledge, if a majority of the board shall so determine; and that express power be given to the local boards to appoint Inspectors of their own to examine in such branches of instruction as the Government Inspectors shall not examine in, and to pay the schoolmaster for giving such instruction from the funds at their disposal; and this power moreover, should also be vested in the managing body of the Normal Schools—(cheers). The Lord Advocate says "we cannot get money for a new endowment of religion;" but his reasoning on this point is very weak. While ostensibly exhibiting the appearance of a desire to defer to the wishes of the people in the matter of religious instruction, he nevertheless endeavours to hoodwink and baulk them with all the ingenuity of the stereotyped special pleader. His argument is, that we will get £70,000 or £80,000 more from the Government grant than at present, and that this should bribe the people into acquiescence—(hear). But, sir, the money does not belong to Mr Young or Mr Forster. That is a pitiful special pleader's fallacy. It is the money of the people the Government is entrusted to administer for the benefit of the people, and, as far as possible, in accordance with their desires. The Government is not in any degree in the position of a donor; it is only giving us a fair share of the funds to which we contribute our full proportion—(cheers). But what does the Lord Advocate mean by a "new endowment of religion?" The words are understood popularly to mean the endowment with public property of a sectarian ecclesiastical corporation, like the Established Churches of Scotland and England; but it is not in this sense a "new endowment of religion" to pay for the religious instruction of the children of Scotland in national schools, in the primary doctrines of the creed of a whole people. He wants to know if we would give the same law to Roman Catholics in Ireland, and doubtless thinks this a very cunning thing to say. But let us examine his proposal. He says he would give to each local board the power to decide as to the religious instruction to be given; and what, I would ask, would a like proposal effect in Ireland? Would it not throw the whole education into the hands of the priests? And even in reference to what he calls the denominational system, denominational grants in Scotland mean a very different thing from what they would be in Ireland, where all such schools would be under the supreme control of the hierarchy, and conducted by ecclesiastics ; but who is it that, he says, stands in the way of our obtaining a Protestant and Scriptural education in our beloved Scotland ? The Lord Advocate tells you that the Pope of Rome forbids them. Where were his blushes when he had the audacity to make such a statement to the Protestant and Christian electors of Galloway ?—(cheers.) The Lord Advocate, with most lamentable obstinacy, still goes in for a London board, obviously with the intention of as soon as possible making the Scotch and English systems alike, which means, of course, dragging our Scotch educational system down to the level of that of England. He says, with charming naivete, that it would be difficult to form a Scotch board. But he does not pretend to say the difficulty is insuperable. We all know that the Lord Advocate is a somewhat indolent senior counsel, and likes all the details to be got up by his junior. The Royal Commission, however, suggested the materials for a Scotch board, and the member for the Universities of Glasgow and Aberdeen suggested another—(hear)—and if the Lord Advocate has not fertility enough to suggest one himself, the plan, sir, I think, would be for him to give up the framing of his Bill to somebody else. When we speak of a representative board in Edinburgh, with its meetings open to the press, we don't mean the sham board to which the Lord Advocate seems to allude; we don't mean a few men without any real power, appointed to perch in a guilded cage, and peck their allowance—(laughter). We mean a permanent board, which will, at least, have the control and initiative in the preparation of the code for Scotland—(hear)—as well as the management which the bill proposes to invest in the so-called Scotch Department of the Privy Council in London. The teacher is so cabined, cribbed, and confined by the code as to make religious instruction well-nigh an impossibility. Unless Scotland has at least the initiative in preparing the code under which the grants are to be given to it, it is ignorant and foolish to say that we have the management of our own schools. Now that we will have an Education Bill for Scotland to settle, this important point of the preparation of the code by ourselves must be strenuously contended for to the very last. The Lord Advocate gives some obviously inaccurate statistics in his speech at Stranraer. He says the numbers who go from the school to the college are in the following proportion—that out of 10,825 scholars only the odd 25 went to college. This, sir, is a very partial and unfair statement. I see it stated that the rolls of the Humanity Class in Edinburgh University show that about 30 per cent of the students of 1865-6 came direct from the Parish, Free Church, and General Assembly Schools ; and I may here say that both the literary and religious character of the schools have been materially injured by the operation of the second code, although in another limited sense it is admitted that it has been beneficial. He says, in another part of his speech, that under the revised code the Inspectors were sent down to Scotland to examine the children in the three R's, and that only a third of those who ought to have passed the examination were able to do so. But I hold the Commission's Report in my hand, second volume, and turning to page 98 I find that the number who passed the second and third standards was about 90 per cent, and those who passed all the standards were, of course, fewer. The Lord Advocate, again, speaks in a most inaccurate way of what he calls the denominational system. In one sense, there is no denominational system in Scotland. The Royal Commission proved that such a thing did not exist, because all denominations attended the schools, and that neither Church of Scotlandism, nor Free Churchism, nor United Presbyterianism, were taught in them. We, of course, admit that schools originating in voluntary liberality, supplemented by Parliamentary grants, would not be of a sufficiently permeating character, and that it would be necessary to engraft on such a system a neutral inspection, to point out any deficiency of education which obtained in any quarter. But this provision could easily be grafted into the voluntary liberality system. If the Lord Advocate cannot secure us a religious national system, the only safe way would be to leave existing agencies alone, and provide for any proved deficiency by rates, local boards, and a compulsory system. This last would be necessary to bring in those children whom the Commissioners describe in large towns as " idling in the streets and wynds, tumbling about the gutters, selling matches, running errands, working in tobacco shops, cared for by no man, with parents or guardians over them who would resent as impertinent interference every care or sympathy that expressed itself in any other way than a gift of money, clothes, or bread." He says he is going to include a compulsory clause, but he does not give us the slightest inkling of what it is to be. The Lord Advocate makes a very ignorant and misdirected sneer at the parish minister. It would have been better taste, and more to the purpose, if he had pointed out some other decided religious influence which was to control the future national schools. But allow me, sir, to allude again to one intended gross interference with the management of our own schools. I refer to the insertion of the odious time-table. This is a mischievous invention, originating in a secular quarter, for the express purpose of reducing religious instruction to the smallest possible minimum. It succeeds in getting religion, in the first instance, pushed into the porch, with the expectation that under its practical operation, in a variety of ways, it would eventually be driven to the street—(cheers). The conscience-clause recommended by the Royal Commission is perfectly sufficient, and all that we can agree to. The difference between the conscience-clause and the time-table may be stated as follows:—By the conscience-clause the child of an objecting parent retires from the religious teaching to do something else in the school. By the time-table the Bible retires from the school, from the continuous education of the day—(hear). By the conscience-clause the individual parent takes the responsibility; by the time-table the nation takes the responsibility, and every one will at once see what a great difference there is between a handful of children retiring from the Bible, and the Bible being made to retire from all the 400,000 or 500,000 children of the schools of Scotland—(loud cheers). It would be an insult, besides, to any teacher worth the having, and who was entitled to our confidence, to ask him to drop his Christian character during the whole period of ordinary teaching, and to purge his school books of all reference to religion, which this odious time-table would of course necessitate—(cheers). With regard to the Irish difficulty in Scotland, the Lord Advocate calculates that there are 4 per cent of Roman Catholics in this part of the kingdom. Could any one, sir, on Scripture grounds, maintain that Christ shall be put out of 96 per cent of our schools, and that they should be thus secularised in the vain and hopeless attempt of keeping antichrist out of 4 per cent of Roman Catholic schools?—(loud cheers). With regard to Ireland, the obvious course to take is to let us have our " use and wont," and to continue in Ireland their " use and wont;" and in regard to Scotland, I wish to remark, in passing, that, as it seems to me, there is no difference in point of principle between Parliament enacting " use and wont," and Parliament deputing a local board to do the same thing. I believe, sir, the week-day schools afford the best, if not only the only opportunity of giving to the greatest number of those who most require it, that religious instruction which is essential to true education—(cheers). And what is very important, children in this way are taught that religion is not a thing only for the Sabbath day, but that it is a divine influence, intended to suffuse and penetrate their hearts in daily life. There is no way of providing a satisfactory substitute for the neglect of religious instruction in the day-schools. To abandon to the Sabbath-school teacher the work of grounding the intellect in the elements of religious knowledge would, in reality, destroy the Sabbath-school; and the Sabbath-school teacher makes very little progress during his hour on Sabbath evening, when the children have not been trained in the facts and doctrines of the Bible in the day-school. Just as it is now well ascertained that the parent is helped, and not hindered, in teaching religion to the child at home by its attendance at the Sabbath-school, so also is it with religious instruction given in the day-school. They both co-operate with the parent in the instruction of his child at home, instead of, as it is sometimes said, interfering with instruction—(hear). But, sir, looking at the state of society around us, we must all agree that it is not only necessary that religion should be taught by the teacher in the day-school, but I believe it to be the grand desideratum of the times; and regarding the matter in a Christian and patriotic point of view, there is hardly anything so important as its revival in all day-schools of every grade, and its being taught in these, more systematically and intelligently than ever. I may notice that it is a great defect in the Lord Advocate's Bill that the securities for the training of teachers by means of Normal Schools which were contained in the Bill of 1869 are left out of it. The " Cheap-John " style in which the Lord Advocate speaks of the teachers is extremely offensive. The office of a teacher is a most responsible one, on public as well as on private grounds. I notice that Mr Potter, who seems to be the " cooper and potter " to the Birmingham League, has kindly intimated that he will do all in his power to bring the curse of a secular system of education upon Scotland; but Scotland, I believe, will prefer the fine gold of her time-honoured Scriptural system to the pinchbeck of Birmingham. As I have already detained you too long, I conclude by reminding you that the Lord Advocate, amidst some misty verbiage, intimates that, " as at present advised," he intends to bring the same Bill in again, which the people of Scotland so universally condemned last year, and which they will, I doubt not, universally condemn this year again, and which we would call an " Instruction Bill," and not on " Education Bill." The sooner the Lord Advocate gets sounder advice the better—at all events, forewarned is fore-armed—and it remains now for us to buckle on our armour for a hand-to-hand fight; raising funds, getting up petitions from every corner, public meetings in every town and village, and arranging for an influential and intelligent deputation to proceed to London to fight the bill every inch of the way, through both houses of Parliament. I trust, sir, by the compact union represented on this platform of all those who are in favour of religious instruction in our schools, we will be enabled, by the help of the Almighty, to fight the battle for the best of blessings to our beloved Scotland—(loud applause).

Dr DAVID EASTON, in seconding the resolution, said—I esteem it a privilege and an honour, Mr Chairman, to be invited to take part in this great meeting in behalf of a religious education in the national schools of Scotland. The character of the Lord Advocate's Education Bill in regard to the common faith of Scotchmen needs only to be exposed to be indignantly condemned and rejected by the nation. The attempt, by a time-table, to prohibit the introduction of Bible teaching into the national education provided by the Bill, seems to me little short of the very climax of anti-religious legislation; and if it be expected that Scotchmen shall stand by and look quietly on, while the splendid heritage which their fathers bequeathed to them is taken away by the despoiling hand of a coalition of discordant powers in which there is yet a temporary unity of unworthy purpose;—then, if her Majesty's Government share that expectation, I trust they shall be speedily undeceived—(applause); for the voice that shall reach them from this and hundreds of other like meetings of resolute Scotchmen may perhaps serve to recal the lesson which Dean Stanley told his Edinburgh audience lately, that all Scottish history conveyed—and the English Parliament may have to learn it yet again—" The motto of your own thistle, ' *Nemo me impune lacessit*,' said the Dean, " might also be rendered in regard to the Scottish Church. None has ever meddled with it without repenting of it"—(applause). The London *Times* recently eulogised Scotland in terms of admiring praise, declaring that it was " the only contented nationality in Europe." I do not wonder that the Scotch have been termed " a peaceable people, far too peaceable, perhaps, in times like these " — (hear, hear, from Dr Begg.) No doubt the Lord Advocate, when framing his Education Bill, was conversant with that fact; but I fear he has presumed too much upon the goodnature of Scotchmen. For when he has enacted in his Bill that the Bible and Bible teaching shall be pushed into a corner of the school, and kept there as a thing to be discouraged and put down, thereby tampering with the very keystone of Scotland's power; and further, that the education so secularised shall be henceforth under the supreme management of a council in London, who can know little or nothing of the Scotch system of education, and who possibly may be less accessible to the influence of the Scotch nation than to that of a certain Cardinal across the channel; —that Scotland shall be deprived of the control of the education of her own children, and subjected to the bye-law regulation of a possibly alien administration;—then it is high time that Scotland's sons speak out, and inform his Lordship that there is a point beyond which their patience may not be taxed, and that it is simply indispensable that the teaching of our common religion continue as heretofore, unfettered and free, and that the principle of the resolution I have now the honour to second be recognised, that " Scotland is entitled to retain in her own hands the management and control of her own schools, which have hitherto proved so great a blessing." Then, and not till then, shall his Education Bill be welcomed by the nation—(much applause).

The resolution was put to the meeting, and carried unanimously.

Rev. Dr BEGG, who rose, amidst loud applause, to propose the third resolution, expressed his great satisfaction at being present at that large and influential gathering of the people of Stranraer. It seemed unnecessary to prolong the meeting after so much had been so well said, and after the unmistakable manifestation of feeling already given. The whole business, however, was not yet disposed of. The resolution he had to propose was as follows:—" That no system of education can be satisfactory which does not secure the proper training, remuneration, and status of the teachers of public schools." He would briefly refer to the resolution, and then also to the more general aspects of the important question that had brought them together. This resolution had reference, first, to the training of teachers. Now, most of them were aware that the training of teachers was a comparatively modern device. There was a time when such things as Normal Schools for the training of teachers had no existence in this country. Men of far greater importance, and who had far greater influence— our members of Parliament—were not trained even yet in Normal Schools, and they were not required to give evidence of their proficiency before entering St Stephen's. He should like to see the one invention introduced as well as the other —(laughter). Meantime they had better retain what they had got, and prevent if they could the removal of their Normal Schools, which had been so great a blessing. One great defect in the Lord Advocate's Bill was that it made no provision whatever for the continuance of Normal Schools. An excellent friend of mine had said that if you do not train the teachers to teach religion, you take the most effectual plan for cutting off the teaching of religion. It was precisely like shutting off gas at the metre—(a laugh)—which would darken the whole town by a single operation. Next, in regard to the remuneration of teachers, that was also of vast importance. In the Lord Advocate's first Bill, as first introduced, there was provision to the extent of the munificent sum of £35 for the teachers, being in full of all the payments which they were to receive—he meant as a minimum. But when the Bill was amended even that provision vanished out of the Bill. Now, the word " amended " in this acceptation afforded a very singular illustration of the use of language, for it proved that they might say that a thing is amended, when, instead of being made better, it was made worse—(laughter). But that was not an unprecedented use of language. There are many similar forms of expression, proving that there is a measure of truth in the idea of Talleyrand that words were invented to conceal ideas. For example, there was nothing more common than to see in their newspapers statements about the Funds. Well, it was just the want of funds. The National Debt was called the Funds, but that was in point of fact just the want of funds—(laughter). And so the Lord Advocate's Bill was said to be amended, when it was, in point of fact, made worse. It had been said—" We must follow the course of demand and supply," and that the principle of free trade must be applied entirely to teachers, in so far as their salaries were concerned. But, unfortunately, the whole of this Bill was framed upon a theory expressly contradictory to the idea of demand and supply. If the theory of free trade had been applied rigidly to the whole matter of education, men would have been left to provide themselves with education or to go without it, just as they pleased. But if they were to introduce a Bill at all for the purpose of providing education, that implied that the principles of free trade were not sufficient to supply the defect—(applause). And if they abandoned the principles of free trade in making a Bill on education at all, they should undoubtedly make the education complete by securing a proper remuneration for the schoolmasters, without which they could not get proper schoolmasters—(applause). It had been confidently said that there is an analogous instance in the case of the rural police to the opposite policy, that a Bill had been passed to make provision for rural police, but not for the payment of them, which is left entirely to the discretion of the counties. But the fact was the very reverse of that, and the Lord Advocate ought to have known it; for, from the Act 20 and 21 Vict., cap. 72, it appeared that the police were not only secured in fixed salaries, but far more liberally paid than even in the unamended Bill would have been the teachers of the youth of Scotland, and if the Bill as it now stood became law, and the other law remained, if he were a schoolmaster he would immediately qualify for being a sergeant of police —(laughter). But what would the probable effect be of having the teachers placed upon the footing of the Lord Advocate's Bill, and that coupled with an imperfect status to the effect that they might be instantly deprived of their position by the mysterious and despotic authority of the Privy Council. They would be virtually also deprived of their characters, for if they were dismissed without trial, simply at the will and pleasure of this party in London, they would have no opportunity of meeting their accusers. The effect would be that, whilst they might get teachers, they would be very different from those they had hitherto had. The Rev. Doctor illustrated this by mentioning a case in point which happened long ago, of a teacher being appointed also session-clerk, precentor, and grave-digger, all to save expense—(laughter). In some districts local boards might, no doubt, still act as economically. The teacher was the school, otherwise, and without good and decently supported teachers, they might bid farewell to education—(applause). By their high character the teachers of Scotland had succeeded in discharging, with much advantage to the country, their high functions, but the moment that state of things ceased that moment the great object of a proper education in Scotland would begin to be defeated—(applause). Dr Begg then went on to speak on the general question, which he said was of vast importance, and in considering it they should begin at the beginning, and ask what it was that entitled or required a Government of a country to provide a system of national education at all? It seemed to be taken for granted that it was the duty of Government to provide a system of national education; and it was further taken for granted that, whilst it was their duty to provide a system of secular education, it was not their duty to provide religious instruction along with it, or as part of it. He should like to hear that first proposition clearly proved, instead of being merely assumed, for among their many sects there were undoubtedly a class of persons not prepared to admit that it is the duty of Government to meddle with education at all, whilst others would say that education was not to be regarded as necessarily a blessing. The first view was formerly maintained by many English Dissenters, and the other view was certainly held by some. Roman Catholics formerly were said to hold that ignorance was the mother of devotion; and he knew that some at least held that ignorance was the mother of obedience on the part of the people. Some time ago, on asking an old heritor of Liberton to subscribe for schools, he was met with the remark, "I'll gae naething ava, for folks were far better when they kenned less"—(laughter). It was said the people ought to be made to know the law, otherwise it was tyranny to punish them for not obeying the law. If they could prove to him, on any ground whatever, that it was the duty of a nation to set up schools at all, he would prove to them far more strongly that it was the duty of the nation to teach the people in the best way, and for the highest purposes to which national education could be turned either here or hereafter—(loud applause). Blackstone told them that Christianity was the foundation of the law of England; and surely, if it were so, the Government of this country, if they taught the people at all, were bound to teach them the foundation of the law, and that Christianity, which is not only the foundation of our law, but the only element of sufficient power to induce the people, by the grace of God, to obey the law. In vain would they tell the people to obey Governments, unless they came to understand that government was a divine ordinance, and to be obeyed, not only for wrath, but also for conscience sake —(hear, hear). It had been said, "You may teach them a great deal of morality without religion." Lying was referred to as a thing that might be deprecated in a school, without reference to religion. In the whole history of the world they could not find an instance in which such mere sentimental secularism had ever had the slightest effect upon the people in inducing them to abstain from any form of sin, because it did not touch their conscience—(applause). They must get at that, otherwise it was vain to speak of the dignity of truth on the one hand, or the meanness of falsehood on the other. Human passion was too powerful for everything and anything but the authority of God and the power of conscience, and no man ought to know that better than the Lord Advocate, because there was not a single witness put into the witness-box that was not obliged to swear with the utmost solemnity. In our courts of criminal law was the Lord Advocate satisfied with saying to the witnesses, " Remember it is a mean thing to tell a lie, and a noble thing to tell the truth "—(laughter). Dr Begg here instanced the case of a woman in Jedburgh, reported in the newspapers two days before, who, on refusing to take the usual oath previous to examination as a witness, was threatened with committal to prison, and, of course, in the event of perjury, she would have been visited with further imprisonment; and he remarked that that was a very different thing from telling her that it was a mean thing to tell a lie—(laughter). The sentimental, mealy-mouthed system which is to be introduced into the schools had, of course, no place in the Lord Advocate's professional practice—(loud applause). The oath also was full of dogmatic points, and took for granted the existence of God, human responsibility, and rewards and punishments; and yet nothing of the sort was to be introduced into the schools; but if the children were not to be taught these things, it was cruelty and tyranny to summon them to courts of Justice, and force them to take such an oath—(loud applause). Therefore, on the ground of their criminal procedure, he held that the theory of teaching morality without religion was refuted by the plainest evidence of facts—(applause). It was technically correct to say that it was not mainly by Acts of Parliament that in a direct form the teaching of religion in our schools was enforced; but still the matter was so arranged by the Legislature as to secure the object. Who laid the foundation of these schools? Every child in Scotland knew that it was John Knox. If we had not had a man in this country called John Knox, humanly speaking, we would not have had that system of education by which we are distinguished from other people—(applause). Why did Knox advocate education at all, and why had they education, while other nations were without it? Exactly because it was necessary for religion. Knox urged the necessity of the godly upbringing of the youth of the realm, so that Christ's cause might be advanced, the best interest of following generations consulted — (applause). From the Act of 1567 down through all the subsequent statutes there was express reference to religion, and to the control of the ministers of religion, in connection with whose control that religious instruction had been enforced to the present day—(applause). If the Lord Advocate had continued and extended the present system, their object would have been secured without more than a distinct recognition of previous statutes and customs as in the Act 1696—(hear). An Act to this effect had passed the House of Commons twenty years ago. Had Parliament grown so much worse since 1852 that this was now said to be impossible ? They had the very thing that was wanted, although not in sufficient quantity just now. Was Government going to take it from them on the pretence that it could not be continued ? He dared them to take it from them. Scotland would rise and resist them if they made the attempt—(great applause). He believed the struggle began originally with the Roman Catholics of Ireland. When the Irish Educational Bill was first discussed, Dr Cook moved and carried the following resolutions :—" 1. That ever since the blessed Reformation, in all the common schools of Evangelical Protestants, but especially in the schools of the Church of Scotland, and in those of the Synod of Ulster and other Presbyterian bodies in Ireland, children have enjoyed the *free and unrestricted use* of the Holy Scriptures, and have been until lately, generally accustomed, where their parents so directed, to learn to read in the sacred volume. 2. That the authoritative exclusion of the Bible from the national schools *during ordinary school hours* seems to have originated, not from any desire of Protestants, but out of deference to the opinions and objections of the Roman Catholic hierarchy, who have always discovered such jealousy and dread of the sacred Scriptures, that wherever they have had the power, they have denied their unrestricted use to the laity in general, and to children in schools in particular ; and farther, that experience demonstrates, that, in whatever country the use of the Scriptures has, in any wise, been restricted, the progress of Protestantism has been proportionably retarded, and the domination of the Church of Rome extended and confirmed." They were then attempting to drive the Bible from the schools in Ireland, and they succeeded in getting it mutilated, and to have extracts from it instead of the whole Book, which Dr M'Crie at the time denounced publicly as a departure from the principles of the Reformation. There was no wonder why the Roman Catholics objected to the Bible : it objected very strongly to them—(laughter). They were like the man mentioned in Scripture, who said, " I hate him, for he never prophesied good of me, but always evil." So Rome wished to repress the Bible because it reflected a very striking light upon her acts and atrocities. Lord Bacon had said that if a hue and cry were sent out for the apprehension of the " Man of Sin," he believed the Pope of Rome would be very speedily apprehended—(laughter). They might take it for granted that Romanism had a special dislike to the use of the Bible. The secularists, again, not only decidedly objected to their own children being taught religion, but to any power being vested in any board to teach religion as part of the national system—(hear, hear). This ground also, for different reasons, was taken of late very strongly by the authorities in the United Presbyterian Church. He was delighted to find that many United Presbyterians sympathised with their movement, and did not agree with their ministers—(applause); but the leading United Presbyterians and the whole synod had given in their adhesion to that principle. In support of this statement, the rev. gentleman quoted from the speech of the Rev. Mr Renton of Kelso, which lately appeared in the *Free Press*; from the resolution adopted in Mr Renton's Presbytery; and from the resolution passed at the last meeting of the United Presbyterian Synod. In that resolution, referring to grants to different bodies, it is said that " all pretext for this provision would be taken away were it declared, as it is clearly implied, that the school rates, like the Parliamentary grants, shall not be applied in respect of any instruction in religious subjects." They had thus the whole United Presbyterian Synod declaring expressly that there shall be no religion supplied in connection with public rates and grants. What did that shut them up to? It shut them up to this —that if any man wished religion taught under the proposed system, he must first of all pay the assessment for the school, and then pay a separate assessment for religion. He put it to every man in that meeting whether it was likely that the parents of the 90,000 destitute children in Glasgow were likely first of all to pay a school rate, and in the second place to be so overwhelmingly anxious for religious instruction that they would pay an additional rate for the purpose of securing it—(loud applause). If they did not do that they would have to go without religious instruction. It was even worse than that, for the precious time-table clause shut out religious instruction during all ordinary school hours. There was here one great difficulty for parents, and another for the children. If a child were to get religious instruction, its parents must pay more than others, and it must start an hour before the school commenced, or remain in school an hour after the school was over, while others were playing in the yard outside. A Scotch schoolmaster in England wrote that the operation of the system there had been most discouraging upon the children, and especially the children of careless parents. People said they must have a division between the teaching of religion and other instruction : that the two things could not be done at once, but the division of the Lord Advocate's Bill would be exactly like the Irishman's division. "Pat," said one Irishman to another, "we must divide the house between us." "Yes," said the other, "I wonder what the division shall be." "Oh," says Pat, "I will get the inside of the house, and you shall get the outside"—(loud laughter and cheers). That was the time-table theory of division : secular instruction was to get the inside, and religious instruction the outside of the school arrangement; but even that was not the worst of it. The schoolroom was upheld by the public rate, and if the voluntary theory was correct they had no more right to use the national schoolroom for religious instruction than they had to use the teacher paid at the public expense—(applause). The religious instruction would therefore become impossible, except on the theory of duplicate schoolhouses, and if they were going to that expense, they might bid goodbye to a national system, and set up their own schools instead of trusting to a broken reed—(applause). Dr Begg then pointed out that they must also eliminate all references to religion from the books used in the schools, that they would not be allowed to use Milton or Shakespeare, and many of our best authors, in them. The whole literature would require to be entirely changed. That was what had taken place in British India in deference to the feelings of the Mahommadans, Hindoos, &c. They had what were called non-Christian books, and the Government prepared them so as to defy all competition. This would probably be the next step here if there was not stout resistance. Such secular books were used also in America, and a minister from this country, on a visit to a school there, was about to mention the name of Jesus, when the teacher said, "Ah, that is the name we must not mention in this school"—(cries of hear, hear). That was what they were coming to in this country. He could show them books recently published which had been changed in the direction of softening or cutting out references to the Reformation and other facts of our national history. They were thus driving on to the purest secularism. There was no middle ground, if the secular or voluntary theory was to be adopted, and he had no hesitation in saying that if such a system was introduced into the schools in Scotland, this country would become as ungovernable as France; perhaps more so, because the Scotch were a more determined people and would thus be far more dangerous—(applause). What had made the great difference between France and this country if it was not the want of religious education? The French otherwise were well educated. Dr Begg quoted the following passage from Robert Hall's splendid sermon on infidelity to prove what might be anticipated if we banished religion from our schools :—" Religion being primarily intended to make men wise unto salvation, the support it ministers to social order, the stability it confers on government and laws, is a subordinate species of advantage which we should have continued to enjoy, without reflecting on its cause, but for the development of deistical principles, and the experiment which has been made of their effects in a neighbouring country. It had been the constant boast of infidels that their system, more liberal and generous than Christianity, needed but to be tried to produce an immense accession to human happiness; and Christian nations, careless and supine, retaining little of religion but the profession, and disgusted with its restraints, lent a favourable ear to these pretensions. God permitted the trial to be made. In one country, and that the centre of Christendom, revelation underwent a total eclipse, while atheism, performing on a darkened theatre its strange and fearful tragedy, confounded the first elements of society, blended every age, rank, and sex in indiscriminate proscription and massacre, and convulsed all Europe to its centre; that the imperishable memorial of these events might teach the last generations of mankind to consider religion as the pillar of society, the safeguard of nations, the parent of social order, which alone has power to curb the fury of the passions, and secure to every one his rights; to the laborious the reward of their industry, to the rich the enjoyment of their wealth, to nobles the preservation of their honours, and to princes the stability of their thrones." He also quoted the following noble passage from the sermon of Dr Chalmers in behalf of the Society for Propagating Christian Knowledge to prove the inestimable importance of Christian training :—" Come and see the effect of her missionary exertions. It is palpable, and near at hand. It lies within the compass of many a summer tour; and tell me, ye children of fancy, who expatiate with delighted eye over the wilds of our mountain scenery, if it be not a dearer and a healthier exercise still to contemplate the habits of her once rugged and wandering population. What would they have been at this moment had schools and Bibles and ministers been kept back from them, and had the men of a century ago been deterred by the flippancies of the present age from the work of planting chapels and seminaries in that neglected land? The ferocity of their ancestors would have come down, unsoftened and un-subdued, to the existing generation. The darkening spirit of hostility would still have lowered upon us from the north; and these plains, now so peaceful and so happy, would have lain open to the fury of merciless invaders. Oh, ye soft and sentimental travellers, who wander so securely over this romantic land, you are right to choose the season when the angry elements of nature are asleep! But what is it that has charmed to their long repose the more dreadful elements of human passion and human injustice? What is it that has quelled that boisterous spirit of her natives? And while her torrents roar as fiercely, and her mountain brows look as firmly as ever, what is it that has thrown so softening an influence over the minds and manners of her living popula-tion?"—the Highlands, where the pennies were put in the letter-box by the wayside for the postman, and the traveller's trunk was left by the passing coach without fear of theft. He concluded: The truth is, we are now brought face to face with the question, are we to give up what has undoubtedly proved so great an advantage to our native land? Are we prepared to give up the Word of God in the schools in Scot-land? What right has England to take from Scotland what she has maintained and used to so much purpose in times past. It is one of the most formidable proposals of despotism I ever heard; for the Parliament, which can control the edu-cation of the country, as an eminent man has said, may do with the country absolutely what it pleases—(hear, hear). We have had many attempts to deprive us of our nationality. We can look back to the time when the Romans invaded Britain, and we know that Scotland remained unconquered when other nations were tramped under foot—that she leaned her back against her stern everlasting hills, and hurled back the imperial power of Rome—(applause). When Edward tried to conquer this country, we have heard of

"Scots wha hae wi' Wallace bled,
Scots wham Bruce had aften led"

—(loud applause). We know that during a later period—and no class of men know it better than you, the children of the Covenanters in this noble southern land of Scotland—(applause)—that the Covenanters foiled a despot's bloody laws, and secured to themselves and to their children that liberty which we now enjoy—(applause). No doubt we have been joined to England, and from the union important ad-vantages have resulted, not only in the cessation of bloodshed, but in a variety of other ways. But England must not seek to neutralise all these advantages by taking away from us what we prize so dear. In fact, if any change is to be made, Scotland had a much better right to propose the establishment of a board in Edinburgh to manage education in England, than England has to demand the management of the education in Scotland—(loud laughter and applause). We are seriously threatened. I stand, I am told, in a peculiar position, at least in this neighbourhood, for I stand nearly alone as the representative of the Free Church ministers. But I glory in the peculiarity, and ask where are the rest?—(hear, and applause). What keeps them back from this noble struggle? I leave an intelligent community to judge. Do they say they agree with us, but they would take a different plan? What is that plan? Let them hold their own meeting and show us their plan—(loud applause). If it be different from ours we will confer with them about it, and if it be the same we will rejoice and go hand in hand with them—(applause). Patriotism requires that every Scotsman should do his duty. I deplore the position of things, but I am not discouraged. I see Scotland rising from Dan to Beersheba—from John o'Groat's to Maidenkirk here—(applause)—and I am certain, by the Divine blessing, that this cause will prosper, because it is the cause of God—(applause). On that memorable occasion to which I have referred Dr M'Crie said—"Scotland, watered by the blood and tears of the martyrs. Am I ashamed of thee? No! but of thy degenerate sons I am ashamed"—(applause). Yes, let us show that we deserve, by the grace and blessing of God, to be considered worthy descendants of the men of the Covenant and the Reformation. Don't let us speak of Knox, and Melville, and Rutherford, and Henderson, and Chalmers, if we do not seek to walk in their footsteps, and hand down, by the Divine blessing, to this noble country of ours, the dear bought and blessed inheritance we have received, lest our children should rise and condemn us when we are silent in the grave—(applause). Let us wave the blue flag of Scripture truth and Reformation principles as long as strength is given to our arms, and when they become paralysed, seek to hand it down with those inestimable blessings it represents to generations yet to come as long as sun and moon endure—(applause). An eminent man has said :—

    "What constitutes a state?
Not high raised battlements, or laboured mound,
    Thick wall or moated gate ;
Not bays or broad-armed ports,
Where, laughing at the storm, rich navies ride ;
    Not starred and sprangled courts,
Where low-browed baseness wafts perfume to pride.

> No ; men, high-minded men,
> With powers as far above dull brutes endued
>   In forests, brake, or den,
> As beasts excel cold rocks and brambles rude ;
>   Men who do their *duties* know,
> But know their rights, and, knowing, dare maintain ;
>   Prevent the long-aimed blow,
> And crush the despot while they rend the chain :
>   These constitute a state."

—(loud and continued applause).

Mr JOHN GIBB seconded the resolution, which was supported by

Mr GORDON, draper, who said,—I have much pleasure in supporting the motion which has been so ably moved by Dr Begg, and all that I would say is, that if you want good teachers you must give them good pay. I would like to speak a word or two on other parts of this great question, and I would say that our country has the best system of education which is to be found in any country in the world. Our system is, that in all our parish and burgh schools the Bible, Shorter Catechism, and secular branches are taught ; and we know that this has been done without any objection, or the slightest confusion, and that for the last three hundred years. There never was the least necessity for time-tables or conscience-clauses. In these schools there are taught Greek, Latin, French, and other branches, along with the Bible and Catechism. A parent is not compelled to have his child taught any of those branches unless he pleases ; so is it with the Bible. Now, I ask every one here who has attended these schools, if ever there was the slightest difficulty in meeting any objections, even religious ones, when they arose. I am sure that all of you will say that you never did. Then I appeal to you and ask, why is this foolish overturn in our educational system demanded ? There is a party in this country whose theory is that the State should not pay for religious teaching, yet by the proposed Bill which has been drawn up by the Lord Advocate to suit their views, when carefully looked into, they will have to pay for religious teaching. The Government is to give £250,000, but only for secular education. Local rates are to yield another large sum, and this party tells us that this money only is to go for secular education. They also tell us that we are to have religious teaching before or after the hours of secular teaching. When asked who is to pay for this religious teaching, they answer that we are to get it into the bargain. Now, we ask them would they have got it into the bargain if they had not paid for the secular teaching ? · They must answer in the negative. After all, they will be paying for religious teaching—(applause). What is the use of demanding such an overturn for a theory which they cannot practically carry out ?—(applause.) This party, again, say, unless we adopt the proposed Bill we will not get an Education Bill for Ireland. Let us get a Bill to answer ourselves, and let the Irish adopt our Bill if they please. We wish Ireland to imitate us, and not us to imitate Ireland. It would be a curious sympathy for us to put off our warm clothing, and put on rags to be like them ; or to begin and pull down our comfortable houses, and put up hovels to be like them. If we were to do these things, people would say we were very foolish. The advice we would give the Irish people and the Government is, put the Bible into every school in Ireland, and the rags and hovels will soon disappear—(applause). A chief from the South Sea Islands asked our excellent Queen what had made her country so great ? She got the Bible, and said this is the book which has done it. Gentlemen, let us unite together and say that the Bible is and must be still taught in our schools—(applause).

The Rev. WILLIAM JOHNSTONE moved the appointment of a committee, with power to add to their number, to promote the object of the meeting, as embodied in the foregoing resolutions, by petitions, deputations, public meetings, and otherwise. He said that at the late hour at which they had arrived it would be out of place to make a speech. Besides, the resolution he had to propose naturally followed those which had been already adopted ; it did not therefore require many words to recommend it. Their enthusiasm had been aroused by the excellent speeches which had been delivered. It was now necessary to carry that spirit into action. They must give effect to the resolutions which had been carried, or what would be the use of their meeting ? Mr Kidston had made use of a happy illustration. He had said that such meetings kindled the heather, lighting a flame which would spread throughout the country, and be seen even across the Border. Now, the heather had been well kindled in Stranraer that night. But the committee which he had to propose must kindle it in other places in the neighbourhood, such as Portpatrick, Cairnryan, and Glenluce. He was delighted to see that they could meet there not as Churchmen, Free Churchmen, United Presbyterians, or Reformed Presbyterians, not as Liberals or Tories, but for a common purpose, and that they could merge their differences in a desire to promote the welfare of the country. He wished the Lord Advocate had been present, that he had seen the earnestness of the various speakers, and the zeal with which the resolutions had been carried. He did not think that he would have gone away with the impression, as he may have done from a former meeting, that in all the provisions of the proposed Education Bill he reflected the opinions of the majority of the electors of Stranraer.

Mr WILLIAM CUMMING, Kirkcolm, seconded the resolution, which was supported by

The Rev. JOHN STURROCK, Stranraer, who said,—I beg, in a few words, to support the resolution which has just been moved and seconded. I sincerely trust and believe that the committee now appointed will be a working committee, and that they will be enabled to do not a little effectively to advance the cause we have all at heart. At this late hour, and after the able, vigorous, and exhaustive speeches to which it has been our privilege to listen, it would be out of place in me to detain the meeting much longer. Permit me, however, to say, that I am glad of the opportunity thus afforded me to express the deep interest which I, in common with many others, feel in this most vital question of National Scriptural Education, and my earnest hope that, notwithstanding all untoward circumstances, the people of Presbyterian, covenanted Scotland will, at this critical juncture in her history, let their voice be heard, demanding what we have this night declared to be essential in any system of education worthy of our country, in such a manner as that none shall dare to refuse it. If they do not— if as a people we do not demand that the fullest legislative security be given that God's truth as revealed in His Word shall continue to be regularly and unrestrictedly taught as heretofore, by men competent to do so, in every school sanctioned and supported by this Protestant nation—then we will show ourselves to be, indeed, the degenerate sons of noble sires, and another proof will be added to the too many already given in our past history, that Ichabod is written on our country—that the glory is speedily departing from this the renowned land of Bibles and of martyrs, and the chosen home of civil and religious liberty. Such meetings as this are to be viewed both with feelings of sorrow and of grateful satisfaction—of sorrow in that they are called for at all, and with gratitude and satisfaction in that, being called for, they are being held, and this, too, with no small success. It is, indeed, to be greatly deplored that our country should be in such a condition as to render necessary such meetings—meetings for the purpose of pressing upon our rulers the duty of legislating on the all-important subject of education in such a way as shall in some adequate measure discharge the solemn national obligations under which we lie to the Bible, and to the God of the Bible. And how has this sad state of things been brought about in our country? How but by our gradual and sinful departing from that high state of civil and ecclesiastical reformation to which our enlightened and patriotic forefathers were honoured of God to raise us as a people. How but through the subtle pernicious influence of that spurious liberalism which is proving one of the deadliest banes of our country—a liberalism which presumes to substitute human will and reason, or rather human caprice, for the will and authority of the Most High speaking in His Word—which aims at obliterating all distinctions of religious belief, placing our reformed religion and Popish error, God's truth and the devil's lie, on the same level—which labours to efface from all our national institutions every memorial of our redemption, and which renounces the supremacy of the Lord Jesus Christ in the very world He created, and which in infinite love He died to save. In connection with this I feel constrained to take the liberty of quoting a few sentences from an able writer lately deceased, which struck me when reading them the other day. Writing upwards of thirty years ago in opposition to the so-called Voluntary principle, " that the magistrate in his official capacity has nothing to do with religion," and in defence of National Religion and Church Establishments, the late Rev. Mr White of Haddington said,—" If the magistrate has nothing to do with religion, then religion ought to be entirely separated from every system of national education. If it be sinful in the magistrate to pay ministers to propagate religion, it must be equally sinful in him to permit this to be done by those teachers who are appointed by Government and supported by a national provision. And only think of the effects that must follow, when common education is separated from religion. If our children are only to be taught to read, to write, and to sum up figures, must they not be a generation of infidels? And will any learning compensate for this? The most intense efforts are presently making to separate religion from common education. Probably on this arena the contest between British Christianity and British infidelity will soon be determined. Let every lover of his children, of his country, and his God, stand up for national education, based upon the Bible." (And so say we now.) "Science without religion is like the waters of Marah without the palm-trees of Elim. When no branch from the tree of life is engrafted on the tree of knowledge, 'its grapes will be grapes of gall, and its clusters bitter.'" Before I sit down, I have another quotation to make, of a very different kind, and a remark or two to pass upon it. Recently the Dean of Westminster made a proclamation in the Greyfriars of Edinburgh, where once the National Covenant of Scotland was sworn and subscribed, and where sleeps the dust of many noble martyrs for Christ's crown and covenant, whose blood was shed by prelatic persecutors; and the proclamation was, that "the Solemn League and Covenant is dead and buried." Now, sir, I regret to have to say that I agree so far with the reverend preacher. The Solemn League and Covenant has, alas! been long buried by the three kingdoms which entered into it; and the learned Dean, in the greatness of his zeal for charity, has done his best to seal it forever in its grave, and to make Scotland believe that the men of the Covenant, who died rather than renounce it at the bidding of prelatic tyranny, were martyrs by mistake. But there is such a thing as being buried alive, and this, I maintain, is what has befallen that noblest and most maligned deed of the fathers of our system of scriptural education, and the founders of our true national greatness. The Solemn League and Covenant has been shamefully buried. But it is not dead—it cannot die. It still lives—aye, and shall live, for its life is of God, whose truth it vindicates and magnifies, and whose glory it seeks to advance. And the time is approaching, we rejoice to believe, when it shall come forth from its grave, and be again joyfully owned and renewed by the humbled, repenting inhabitants of these realms as the precious charter of their dearest liberties, and as one of the grandest instruments for promoting the interests of the Redeemer's kingdom, and the highest welfare of our beloved land. And when that happy time arrives—and may it come speedily—there will be no occasion for such meetings as this to do battle in behalf of the sacred cause of the godly upbringing of the young in the schools of the nation, for then by us as a nation shall that blessed word be willingly honoured which God Himself has magnified above all, His name.

Rev. THOMAS EASTON said :—I beg to move that this meeting accord a vote of thanks to the deputation who have this evening honoured us with their presence—(applause)—and who have so admirably responded to our invitation, by the able addresses they have now delivered—(applause). The provisions of the Lord Advocate's Education Bill, in so far as it recognises the duty of the State to educate the youth of the land, but refuses to make that education religious—declaring that it shall be exclusively and continuously secular—is simply voluntaryism removed from the regions of abstraction, and embodied in the concrete form of national rebellion against the authority of God and his Word—(applause). And, therefore, I do not wonder when I find an eminent Free Church minister —I allude to the Rev. Dr Candlish—saying, in quite recent times, for it was years after the Disruption, that "a prospect of a good national scheme of education never dawns upon us but voluntaryism steps in to bar and render it impossible "— (applause). But Scotland, I think, is now beginning to shake herself free from the political trammels of an infidel political theory. When I look at this large and enthusiastic meeting, and consider its generally representative character, I think I may venture to convey to that deputation the assurance that the Scots of Galloway, ably led in this district by our distinguished Chairman—(cheers)—shall not be wanting in the advocacy of the Godly upbringing of the youth of this land; and, therefore, I move that to the Chairman, as well as to the deputation, the hearty thanks of this meeting be accorded— (great cheering.)

The CHAIRMAN acknowledged the vote, and said he trusted the committee would go forward to the work assigned them, with deliberation, care, and anxiety, to further the cause of the meeting, and that it would not merely end in empty enthusiasm—(applause).

The Rev. Mr STURROCK then pronounced the benediction, and the meeting separated shortly after ten o'clock, the proceedings having occupied three hours.

APPENDIX.

THE EDUCATION QUESTION AND THE LORD ADVOCATE.

(From the " Galloway Gazette," January 13, 1872.)

LECTURE AT STRANRAER.

THE Rev. T. Easton, Stranraer, delivered a lecture in his own Church last Wednesday evening, on the Education Question, with special reference to the speech of Lord Advocate Young delivered in Stranraer last week. There was a large and influential attendance notwithstanding the severity of the weather.

Mr EASTON began by declaring his conviction that they had now arrived at a solemn crisis in the history of their country, and that it was the duty of every Christian-minded Scotchman to do what he could to resist the daring attempt of the Lord Advocate and his political friends to revolutionise and secularise the whole system of Scottish Education by obtaining a decree of the empire that henceforth the Word of God shall be excluded from the National Education of all the National Schools of Scotland. The Lord Advocate had propounded an Education Bill which was simply one of unmitigated secularism—(applause). He knew the Lord Advocate had a difficult part to act the other evening. So recently as last March the inhabitants of Stranraer, assembled in public meeting, under the presidency of their Provost, had condemned, with singular energy of expression, his godless scheme—(applause)—and, therefore, with the graceful tact of the accomplished pleader who knows that he is addressing an adverse jury, he took care to veil the odious and repulsive announcement he had to make with the gaudy drapery of some welcome sentiment. Accordingly, at becoming intervals, he interspersed his address with some such piety as this—that " a child without religious knowledge is not educated, even elementarily, in such a manner as to fit him for his duties in the world, in any station, however humble ;" and again, " any measure which offered a hindrance to the religious education of the young would be an offence against the sense and the feeling of the people of this country, of which he for one would not willingly be guilty." But the announcement itself, however hateful to his audience, he could not withhold; and, therefore, with creditable explicitness, he said that " that which he proposed last year it was his intention to propose again to Parliament this year;" and therefore, that the education provided by the Government shall be secular—that in every national school the secular education shall be continuous—that no religious instruction throughout the whole period of the educational day shall be tolerated by Government; in short, that secular education shall be the only education for which the Government will legislate, the only education the Government Inspector will examine, and the only education for which the Government will pay. That is the sort of education for which our present system, which has stood the test for centuries, is to be overthrown that it may be substituted in its stead. What, then, could the Lord Advocate hope to gain by attempting to bamboozle his audience with the statement " that no impediment of any kind shall be offered to the people of this country in respect to the religious instruction of their children?" What greater impediment could be offered than that which the Bill enacted? There is no greater impediment conceivable in legislative enactment aside of the impossible legislation which would re-enact the tyranny of the Stuarts, and require another Claverhouse to enforce —(applause).

NO MORE ENDOWMENTS.

But the Lord Advocate proceeded to assign a reason for his refusal of religious instruction to the people. " The time has gone by," he said, " for any new endowments or establishments for religion." What were the facts? When they disestablished the Irish Protestant Church did not the Government, of which the Lord Advocate is a distinguished member, effect the establishment, in perpetuity, of the Popish College at Maynooth?—(applause). Since that time had they not passed another Endowment Bill, by which every Popish priest in Ireland is endowed with money and land,—ten acres of a glebe,—under cover of a loan to all ecclesiastical bodies in that country?—(applause). Will his Lordship tell them what part he took in nineteen different attempts which the Government made last year to force on the Prison Ministers Bill, by which a Popish priest would have been established as an endowed chaplain, at a salary ranging from £25 to £200 per annum, in every jail in the kingdom where ten or more Popish prisoners were confined?— (cheers). Did not one of the most zealous supporters of the present Government—a gentleman who calls himself a "staunch Liberal," and who is one of the most distinguished of the Scottish Voluntaries —tell his own Presbytery at Kelso the other week, in terms of unaffected dismay, that "the system of endowments, instead of being abrogated, or arrested, or abated, is persisted in, fostered, and augmented by the policy of the Government, until now the country is threatened with a deluge of new religious establishments, among which Episcopacy and Popery shall obtain revived domination by State support?" The time for any new endowments or establishments of religion gone by! The idea is but the hallucination of some ill-informed and over-sanguine Voluntary, or the clever device of some guileful political schemer—(cheers). The disendowing and disestablishing tendency of the times *is* a fact, but thanks to a so-called Liberal Government, it is the disendowing and disestablishing of Protestant Christianity, and the endowing and establishing of Popery in its stead—(applause).

SOME RELIGION LEFT IN THE SCHOOLS.

The Lord Advocate palliated his purposed legislative expulsion of the Bible from the National Schools of Scotland by telling us that, after all, there will be some religion left. His words were that "a certain piety shall accompany all the efforts of the schoolmaster in teaching the young; that he shall use legitimate occasion to instruct the mind and the heart of a child in those things not involving any doctrinal questions at all, or any teaching of religion in that sense which gives occasion to controversy; that he shall teach it how wrong, not in the sight of man only, but in the sight of God —how mean, how cowardly, falsehood is; how noble and generous truth is; and impress it with all those views which are calculated to instruct its mind and its heart, and keep it straight in its course through life; and so far as they attain that result, they do not come within the category of teaching religion at all." Wonderful law, and yet more wonderful Gospel! The Bible is shut out of the school, and yet all this religion is kept in it! Judge Storer, of the Supreme Court of Cincinnati, not long ago, pronounced the judgment of the court to the effect that it is not in the power of an American school board to interdict the teaching of the Word of God in the public schools of America. When the case was argued before the court, one of the counsel had used the following argument:—"That when the Constitution says religion and morality and knowledge are essential to good government, it simply means that the intuitive sense of right and wrong shall be wrought out by exercise and developed; the only religion that it considers vital to the preservation of the State is that which is written upon human nature." Now, this argument seems to closely resemble the logical and theological plea of the Lord Advocate, when he tells us that, though the Bible be legislated *out* of the school, yet religion and morality may be legally taught *in* it. It is not, therefore, an unbecoming thing to ask the Lord Advocate to listen to the reply—he might call it a rebuke—which his Transatlantic brother, of a position professionally as high as his own, thus addresses to him :—" Without the teachings of the Holy Scriptures there is no unvarying standard of moral duty, no code of ethics which inculcates willing obedience to law, and establishes human governments upon the broad founda- tion of the Will of God. Religion is necessary to good govern- ment, not the shadowy view of man's duty, which lets in upon the vision a faint ray of light to make the surrounding darkness more visible, but the recognition of an Almighty Power, demonstrable, it is true, by what meets our vision, but alone subjectively taught by His revealed will. Yet it is said the natural conscience is to be taught, the instinctive sense of right and wrong is to be brought out by exercise and developed ; but we are not told what is to be the exercise, or how the development is to be effected ;—what is to be the process by which the minds of the young are to be cast into the crucible and refined from any innate or acquired impurity ;— what high and holy motive is to be addressed to the pupil when his origin, the purpose of his probation on earth, and all knowledge of a hereafter are not only to be withheld, but the volume which discloses them is ostracised as one not only unfit to be read, but as conflicting with the conscience that has never yet, perhaps, been enlightened by its truth "—(applause).

DENOMINATIONAL TEACHING.

But the Lord Advocate told us that it was doctrinal teaching which he would interdict—"that teaching which distinguishes one Church from another." But there was no such thing as denomi- national teaching in the schools of Scotland. The implied allegation on which the Lord Advocate grounded his proposed subversion of their Scottish education was utterly untrue. A distinguished ex- Moderator of the General Assembly of the Church of Scotland, at a public meeting in Montrose last week, applied to that allegation the energetic corrective that "*it was a downright falsehood.*" The fact was that the Royal Commission, appointed in 1864, examined forty witnesses, and every one of them agreed in testifying that there was no such thing as denominational teaching in Scottish schools ; and yet, on the plea of preventing denominationalism, the Lord Advocate interdicts the Bible—(applause).

PRIVY COUNCIL MANAGEMENT.

Mr Easton next referred to the question of a Scottish board, and quoted approvingly the declaration of Sir Wm. Gibson-Craig at the Edinburgh County Meeting last year, when he said that " there ought to be a most resolute determination that Scotland should have a proper working board in Edinburgh, composed of men who understood the Scotch system thoroughly, and who had devoted their lives to the consideration of the ways in which our present good system might be still further improved. If the management of the measure was to be put into the hands of a London board, he would rather see the Bill thrown out altogether, because it would be utterly impossible for such a board to work it efficiently. On that ground alone he held it was absolutely necessary to protest against the Bill." It was gratifying to the people of Galloway to observe that the Earl of Stair was present at that meeting, and that, with a patriotic concern for the best interests of his country, he gave his powerful support to Sir Wm. Gibson-Craig, and voted for the motion which embodied his protest against the Bill—(cheers).

REMUNERATION OF TEACHERS.

Mr Easton next considered the subject of the remuneration and status of teachers, and unsparingly condemned, amid loud applause, the reasonings by which the Lord Advocate sustained his contemptuous treatment of them. Ninety thousand children in Scotland, he said, were growing up in ignorance and vice. To remedy the evil, a compulsory education was to be enacted; and yet the remuneration of the teachers, like that of the "Glasgow scavengers," to whom his Lordship tastefully alluded, was to be left to the operation of the law of supply and demand!

THE IRISH DIFFICULTY.

"I should like," said the Lord Advocate, "just to ask those who support the proposal about which I have been speaking"—the proposal for a scriptural education—"whether they are prepared to ask the Government to support the passing of a measure for Ireland, that in the national schools of Ireland, maintained at the public expense, the Roman Catholic religion, and that only, should be taught by the schoolmasters?" Such a question from a member of Her Majesty's Government—one of the chief officers of the nation, the very foundations of whose constitution are Protestant, is certainly rather startling. If Protestant Christianity be taught in Scotland, then Popery must be taught in Ireland! Because the Papists of Ireland refuse the Word of the living God, therefore, in the name of political justice, must it also be withheld from the Protestants of Scotland! It is written of those who would do evil that good may come that "their damnation is just." The argumentation of the Lord Advocate, if it had been correctly reported, has been well characterised as that of a "satanic logic"—(applause). It is a scandal to the Protestants of Scotland that such impious doctrine should be flaunted before them in face of day—(loud cheers).

NO LAW FOR RELIGIOUS EDUCATION.

But the Lord Advocate told them that "there is no law prescribing the teaching of religion in the schools at present." The Lord Advocate was surely forgetting some of the facts of their Scottish history. Could it be that the Act passed by the Scottish Estates in 1696, establishing the parochial school system with such guarantees of religious management as secured a religious education that was distinctively a Christian and Protestant education, had been overlooked by his Lordship? Or is it forgotten that in 1560 —the very year when Popery was abolished—the first Protestant

General Assembly of the Church of Scotland addressed to the great Council of Scotland, in the form of a solemn message, this fervent expostulation and appeal :—"It is of necessity that your honours be most careful of the virtuous and godly upbringing of the youth of this realm," and that resulting from that appeal, there came, in due time, the glorious privileges of a settled Christian National Education, which for centuries has been the glory of their land—(loud applause).

THE GLADSTONE GOVERNMENT CHARACTERISED.

A distinguished Scottish Voluntary—he alluded to Rev. Mr Renton—and therefore no unduly prejudiced observer of the facts and tendencies of British legislation, has recently declared respecting the Government of this country, that "in relation to religious liberty, in respect for religion, in regard for the rights of conscience, the policy of that Government, since its great measure of disestablishing the Irish Church, has been not only inconsistent, but retrogressive and scandalous ;" and when he (Mr Easton) looked to the secularistic, and Voluntary, and pro-Popish measures of their administration, and listened to the authoritative exposition, by the Lord Advocate, of their godless educational scheme with its threatened pendant of national degradation, he felt constrained, by the survey, to declare his conviction that perhaps a worse Government has not occupied the place of power since the days of Bolingbroke. But when he further considered that

> "The ancient spirit is not dead,
> Old times, methinks, are breathing still,"

he trusted that this latest affront to Scottish faith would speedily provoke, from the united voice of the people, the same appeal their fathers made in the early times of the Reformation to the great Council of Scotland, but which shall now be addressed to the great Council at Westminster—an appeal that shall be spoken with the emphasis of an earnest nation, "It is of necessity that your honours be most careful of the virtuous and godly upbringing of the youth of this realm"—(loud cheers).

CONCLUSION.

Mr Easton concluded an address, which occupied upwards of an hour in the delivery, by reading the following sentences from a speech of the late Dr Chalmers, spoken amid the intense enthusiasm of a great Edinburgh meeting :—" It was religion in Scotland which gave the first impulse to education—(cheers). John Knox and his associates—(loud cheers)—convinced the popular understanding of the country that the Bible was the genuine record of communication from God to man, and that within the four corners of that Book there were the words which were able to make them all wise unto salvation. It was this which inspired them with a universal desire to possess the faculty of reading, that they might unlock the mysteries of the Scriptures, and acquire the knowledge of God, and of His Son Jesus Christ, which is life everlasting. It was this which created a universal demand for education among the people of Scotland—(cheers). Therefore, we ought never to forget that religion is the parent of our schools—that if these schools, by an act of unnatural rebellion, should cast off the authority of their parent—if they should ever forget and disown their great progenitor to whom they owe their birth and their being—all the blessings and glory which they ever conferred on our land will speedily depart from it—(cheers). By the wretched exchange of the bread of life for the mere husks of unsanctified knowledge the moral health of the young and rising generation would wither to extinction, just as surely as would their physical health, if they were bereft of the proper nourishment of man, and driven to the wretched necessity of feeding on ashes. I confess that I look with a great degree of jealousy and dislike on all the tamperings, on the part of crude and incompetent speculators, with the sacred business of education—(loud cheers). The proposal to take the Bible from the school, if it is not just like dropping poison into the fountain-heads of our national morality, is at least taking away from those fountain-heads the healing waters of the sanctuary—(cheers). Our people would indeed continue to be taught, but the light put before them would be moral darkness ; and we have the authority of our Saviour for saying how great would be that darkness—(cheers). Knowledge, it is said, is power, and if knowledge is associated with religion, it becomes a power for the virtuous and the good, and tells with the best and most beneficent influence on the well-being of society. But if knowledge be dissociated from religion, this destroys not the truth of the maxim that knowledge is power, but then it is power emancipated from the restraints of principle, and such a power let loose upon society, like the deep policy of an artful tyrant, or the military science of a ruthless conqueror, would have only the effect to enslave and destroy—(loud cheers). Yes, gentlemen, we mean to have our schools ; but we mean, in the economy of these schools, to abide by the good old ways of our forefathers—(cheering). We mean to have the Bible the regular and daily school-book—(cheers). We mean to have the Catechism for a regular and daily school exercise—(cheers). And these shall be taught openly and fearlessly, not dealt with as contraband articles—(cheers). Not smuggled into a mere hole and corner of our establishment. Not mended or mutilated by human hands, that the message of the Eternal may be shaped to the taste and the prejudices of men—(cheers). Not confined to the odd days of the week, or made to skulk from observation into a bye-room, lest the priests of an intolerant faith should be offended—(loud cheering). No, gentlemen, we will place the Word of God in the forefront of our system of education—(cheering). And we will render it the unequivocal, the public, the conspicuous object that is becoming a Christian and Protestant nation "—(cheers).

MEMBERS OF COMMITTEE.*

Balmer, Rev. Stephen, Portpatrick.
Barty, Rev. Thomas, Kirkcolm.
Birch, Major-General, Dunskey.
Bisset, Thomas, Stranraer.
Bryson, George, Stranraer.
Clanachan, Andrew, Allandoo.
Cochran, John, Portencallie.
Cluckie, Neven, Stranraer.
Cowan, George, Mains of Park.
Cumming, William, Kirkcolm.
Dalrymple, The Right Hon. Viscount.
Donnan, George, Stranraer.
Dougall, Rev. James, Stoneykirk.
Douglas, William, Liddesdale.
Douglas, John, Mark.
Douglas, John, Auchmantle.
Drynan, Andrew, Glenapp.
Easton, Rev. T., Stranraer.
Easton, Dr David, Stranraer.
Easton, Dr James, Stranraer.
Forsyth, Rev. William, New Luce.
Frederick, Andrew, Clendry.
Frood, Rev. Bryce, Glenluce.
Gellie, Rev. James C., Leswalt.
Gibb, William, Stranraer.
Gibb, John, Stranraer.
Gibson, Rev. Henry, Glenapp.
Gordon, John, Stranraer.
Hay, Admiral Sir J. C. D., of Dunragit, Bart.
Johnman, Rev. John, New Luce.
Johnston, Rev. Wm. M., Stranraer.
Kennedy, James, South Cairn.
Kennedy, William, Knocktim.
Kennedy, Charles, Glengyre.
Kelly, Charles, Stranraer.
Kerr, Charles, Larbrax.
Lawrie, James, Inch.
Leslie, Wm. Marshall, Newton-Stewart.

Lupton, Robert, New Luce.
Lusk, Peter, Craigcaffie.
Martin, William, Larbrax.
Millar, Archibald, Stoneykirk.
Milroy, John, Balgreggan.
Morland, Thomas, Lochnaw.
M'Clew, John, Dinvin.
M'Cornack, Dr W., Glenluce.
M'Caig, Peter, Mye.
M'Caig, John, Boreland.
M'Cosh, Peter, Cairngaan.
M'Crae, Archibald, Half Mark.
M'Credie, John, Drummuckloch.
M'Douall, Colonel, Logan.
M'Gibbon, William, Stranraer.
M'Harg, Alexander, Cairnside.
M'Harg, Alexander, Glenapp.
M'Intyre, Charles, High Curghie.
M'Kie, Alexander, Stranraer.
M'Lean, Thomas, Stranraer.
M'Lellan, Alexander, Balyett.
M'Millan, James, Enoch.
M'Walker, Andrew, Gleniron.
Orgill, Dr John, Stranraer.
Parker, John, Inchparks.
Ralston, John, Milmain.
Rankin, Alexander, Aird.
Stewart, Mark J., Ardwell.
Shaw, David, Stranraer.
Symington, Gilbert, Glenluce.
Sturrock, Rev. John, Stranraer.
Todd, John, Auchleach.
Todd, William, Auchness.
Wallace, Sir William T. F. A., of Lochryan, Bart.
Williamson, Rev. W., Kirkmaiden.
Wither, James, Awhirk.
Wylie, Joseph, Stranraer.

* This Committee includes Ministers and Elders of each of the Presbyterian Churches of Scotland.